James T. Bradley, Maurice Clabaugh

Manual of Elocution for Use in County Normal Institutes and Graded and Common Schools

James T. Bradley, Maurice Clabaugh

Manual of Elocution for Use in County Normal Institutes and Graded and Common Schools

ISBN/EAN: 9783337780135

Printed in Europe, USA, Canada, Australia, Japan

Cover: Foto ©Thomas Meinert / pixelio.de

More available books at **www.hansebooks.com**

MANUAL

OF

ELOCUTION

FOR USE IN

COUNTY NORMAL INSTITUTES,

AND

GRADED AND COMMON SCHOOLS.

PREPARED BY

JAMES T. BRADLEY AND MAURICE CLABAUGH.

SEDAN, KANSAS.

PREFACE.

We issue the Manual of Elocution in order to supply common and graded school teachers with something complete, concise and cheap upon the subject. It furnishes an easy, progressive and natural introduction to the science and art of one of the most enchanting and entertaining accomplishments.

The subject is treated in twenty lessons, containing such subject matter and arranged in such manner as to not only render a knowledge of Elocution a pleasure and pastime to acquire, but to suggest an effective method of teaching it.

Our drills are simple and appropriate for examples and indispensible for illustrating the different parts of the subject; our outline is logical and complete as far as this treatise extends, and cannot fail to present the subject in a tangible light; our selections for practice are at once interesting to read and study, and adapted to an application of the principles taught.

We gratefully acknowledge our indebtedness to Mr. Townsend, whose inimitable Seventy Lessons in Civil Government suggested a distribution of our outline throughout the work; to Messrs. Hamill and Shoemaker, whose books we often consulted, and to Mr. Bacon for his valuable suggestions on Gesture.

Twenty Lessons in Elocution.

LESSON I.

1. Elocution is the natural expression of thought by means of speech and gesture.

By Natural is meant our highest or God-given nature, and implies the highest attainment to which the individual is capable. By Expression is meant a conveyance, or giving out of impressions. By Thought is meant the product of mental operations, and embraces concepts or ideas, passion or sentiment. By Speech is meant every intelligent use of the organs of utterance, whether articulate or inarticulate, whispered or vocal. By Gesture is meant attitude, movements of the limbs, and facial expression.

2. Three objects of Elocution.
1. To understand what is read.
2. To give proper expression to what is read.
3. To give mental and physical culture.

It is desirable to Understand what is read, in order—First, to get a clear idea of the meaning to be conveyed by the author; and, Second, to extend the knowledge of the student. In order to give proper Expression to what is read, it is necessary for the student:

First. To pronounce and define the words.

Second. To explain the meaning of the language.

Third. To determine what is beautiful and good in sentiment.

Fourth. To give reasons for the manner of delivery.

It is not absolutely necessary to understand what is read to have a good delivery, for by imitation we may reach a good degree of perfection on a particular selection, but without understanding there will be no increase of knowledge, and we will never be able to read other selections well than the ones learned by imitation; therefore, the practice of teaching by imitation is to be condemned, for the reason that it destroys the individuality of the pupil by depriving him of Mental Culture, and substituting the mechanical for the natural.

By Mental Culture is meant the acquisition of knowledge, cultivation of taste, and training of judgment; and by Physical Culture is meant such a development of the vocal organs and movements of the body as will give ease and grace to delivery.

3. Principles.
1. Speech.
2. Gesture.

4. The Principles of Elocution embrace Speech and Gesture.

By Principles is meant a ground of action, or fundamental truth. It is evident that a fundamental truth of Elocution is that the art consists of Speech and Gesture; for by Speech is given the proper Utterance, Articulation and Modulation; and by Gesture is given the proper Attitude, Movements of Limbs, and Facial Expression.

    1. Commit the definition of Elocution.
    2. Read carefully the explanation of the definition.
    3. Commit three objects of Elocution.
    4. Read carefully the explanation of the objects.
    5. Commit the two divisions of the Principles and learn the Outline.
    6. Read carefully the explanation of the Principles.

QUESTIONS.

    1. What is Elocution?
    2. What are the three objects of Elocution?
    3. Place the outline of divisions on the blackboard.
    4. What are the two divisions of the Principles?

LESSON II.

5. Speech. $\begin{cases} \text{1. Articulation.} \\ \text{2. Utterance.} \\ \text{3. Modulation.} \end{cases}$

6. Speech is the means of communicating thought by the vocal organs.

The nature of man requires that he should have an extensive language. The strongest evidence of this is that he has faculties, which enable him to acquire a knowledge of language, and speech, which enables him to use it. The wisdom of the ages might search all departments of nature for a more perfect and sufficient means of exchanging thought than by Speech, but the search would be vain. Its value and efficiency consists in its double relation—*to self and to others.* The mind would become a Dead Sea, with no outlet, if it were not for language; its thoughts would become stagnant and self-devouring if it were not for Speech.

It is very essential that ones' vocabulary be as extensive as the utmost demands of his avocation require; that his vocal organs be thoroughly cultured, so that his Speech may have that degree of beauty and power of which it is capable.

7. The three elements of Speech are Articulation, Utterance and Modulation.

8. Articulation.
  { 1. Vocal Sounds.
  { 2. Breath Sounds.
  { 2. Union Sounds.

9. Articulation is the distinct utterance of Elementary Sounds.

By *distinct utterance* is meant such pure, clear, round tones as will give language its full beauty end power.

10. The three classes of Articulate Sounds are Vocal, Breath and Union.

11. The Vocal Sounds are those which are unobstructed by the organs of utterance, and consist of tone.

12. Breath Sounds are those which consist of mere emissions of breath.

13. Union Sounds are those which consist of breath and tone, modified by the organs.

1. Commit the definition of Speech.
2. Read carefully the explanation of Speech.
3. Commit the three elements of Speech, and learn the outline.
4. Commit the definition of Articulation, and learn the outline.
5. Read carefully what is said in explanation of the pefinition of Articulation.
6. Commit the three classes of Articulate Sounds.
7. Commit the definition for Vocal, Breath and Union Sounds.
8. Practice on the following exercises in Breathing and Articulation :

Breathing ..
  { Slowly. { Stand erect. Take full and deep inhalntions. Exhale slowly.
  {   { Chest breathing. Abdominal breathing. Alternate.
  { Forcibly.. { Stand erect. Take full and deep inhalations and exhalations.
  {   { Pant on the sound of H. Puff forcibly and quickly.

Cab'n	for cab-*i*n.		Wil-ler	for wil-lo*w*.
Barr'l	for bar-r*e*l.		Chil-drin	for chil-dr*e*n.
Ev'ry	for ev-*e*-ry.		Per-ta-ter	for po-ta-to.
Hist.ry	for his-*to*-ry.		Wind-er	for win-do*w*.
Par-tic'lar	for par-tic-*u*-lar.		Gov-er-ment	for gov-er*n*-ment.
Prince	for prints.		Prod-*u*.*x*	for prod-u*c*ts.

Let us hope   instead of Let us soap.
He had two small eggs   "   " He had two small legs.
Bring some ice cream   "   " Bring some I scream.
She told her age   "   " She told her rage.
Science and art   "   " Science an' dart.

She sells sea shells.

She shuns sunshine ; do you shun sunshine?

A big black bug bit a big black bear.

He adds fourths, fifths, sixths, sevenths, eighths, ninths and tenths with skill.

Masses of immense magnitude move majestically through the vast empire of the solar system.

QUESTIONS.

5. Place the outline of Speech on the blackboard.
6. What is Speech?
7. What are the three elements of Speech?
8. Place the outline of Articulation on the blackboard.
9. What is Articulation?
10. What are the three classes of Articulate Sounds.
11. What are Vocal Sounds?
12. What are Breath Sounds?
13. What are Union Sounds?

LESSON III.

14. Utterance. $\begin{cases} \text{Form.} \\ \text{Quality.} \end{cases}$

15. Utterance is the act of producing speech.

16. The divisions of Utterance are Form and Quality.

17. Form. $\begin{cases} \text{Effusive.} \\ \text{Expulsive.} \\ \text{Explosive.} \end{cases}$

18. Form is the manner in which the sound issues from the vocal organs.

19. The three classes of Form are Effusive, Expulsive and Explosive.

20. The Effusive Form is that in which the sound issues forth in a smooth, gentle manner, without abruptness.

The Effusive Form is naturally adapted to expressions of pathos, reverence, awe, solemnity, devotion and adoration.   The sighing of the wind, the distant rolling of the thunder, the ceaseless moaning of the ocean, are all in the Effusive.   The elevating and ennobling aspirations and sentiments of the soul are expressed in the Effusive Form.

1. Learn the outline of Utterance.
2. Commit the definition of Utterance.
3. Learn the divisions of Utterance.

4. Learn the outline of Form.
5. Commit the definition of Form.
6. Learn the three classes of Form.
7. Commit the definition of Effusive Form.
8. Read carefully the explanation of Effusive Form.
9. Drill on the Effusive Form with the following examples:

Effusive
{
"O, that I had the wings of a dove that I might fly away and be at rest."
"Roll on, thou ever deep and dark blue ocean, roll."
"O, thou Eternal one! whose presence bright all space doth occupy."
"The curfew tolls the knell of parting day."
}

QUESTIONS.

14. Place the outline of Utterance on the blackboard.
15. What is Utterance?
16. What are the divisions of Utterance?
17. Place the outline of Form on the blackboard.
18. What is Form?
19. What are the classes of Form?
20. What is Effusive Form?

LESSON IV.

21. The Expulsive Form is that in which the voice issues forth in a forcible manner, with more or less abruptness.

This Form is used in the various kinds of public address, which are delivered with force and emphasis. It is used by the lawyer when advocating his cause, by the legislator when addressing the assembly, by the lecturer on the rostrum, and by the politician on the platform.

1. Commit the definition of Expulsive Form.
2. Learn what expressions are naturally adapted to the Expulsive Form.
3. Read carefully the explanation of of the Expulsive Form.
4. Review the drill on Effusive Form.
5. Drill on the Expulsive Form with the following examples:

Expulsive
{
"There is her history, the world knows it by heart."
"Three millions of people armed in the holy cause of liberty."
"Let no man dare, when I am dead, to charge me with dishonor."
"O, I have passed a miserable night. so full of fearful dreams."
}

QUESTIONS.

21. What is the Expulsive Form?

2

LESSON V.

22. The Explosive Form is that in which the voice issues forth instantaneously.

The voice naturally assumes this form in vocal response to sudden impulses of the mind. Abrupt outbreaks of passion and sentiment are expressed in the Explosive Form. The quick crack of the rifle, the startling crash of the thunderbolt, the passionate outburst of laughter, are all examples of this form.

1. Commit the definition of Explosive Form.
2. Learn what expressions are adapted to the Explosive Form.
3. Read carefully what is said in explanation of the Explosive Form.
4. Review the drills on Effusive and Expulsive Forms.
5. Drill on Explosive Form with the following examples:

Explosive
{
"Fire! Fire! Put out the fire!"
"Arm! arm! it is—it is the cannons opening roar."
"Strike! till the last armed foe expires!"
"Charge! Chester, charge! On! Stanley, on!"
}

QUESTIONS.

22. What is the Explosive Form?

LESSON VI.

23. Quality.
{
1. Pure.
2. Orotund.
3. Aspirate.
4. Pectoral.
5. Guttural.
6. Nasal.
7. Falsetto.
}

24. Quality is the kind of tone.

25. There are seven kinds of tone: Pure, Orotund, Aspirate, Pectoral, Guttural, Nasal and Falsetto.

26. Pure Quality is the simplest use of the vocal organs.

It is suited to language of plain description, ordinary conversation and simple narrative.

27. Orotund Quality is the Pure Quality enlarged and deepened.

It is suited to expressions of reverence, awe, adoration and other varieties of sublime thought.

1. Learn the outline of Quality,
2. Commit the definition of Quality.
3. Learn the classes of Quality.
4. Commit the definition of Pure Quality.
5. Commit the definition of Orotund Quality.
6. Learn to what expressions each are adapted.
7 Drill on Pure and Orotund Quality with the following examples

Effusive... { Pure—"The day is cold, and dark, and dreary."
Orotund—"Thou too, sail on, oh! ship of state, sail on.'

Expulsive { Pure—"I said an elder soldier, not a better."
Orotund—"It is in vain, sir, to extenuate the matter."

Explosive { Pure—I'O! I'O! They come! they come!
Orotund—Rouse ye, Romans! rouse ye, slaves!

QUESTIONS.
23. Place the outline of Quality on the blackboard.
22. What is Quality?
25. What are the classes of Quality?
26 What is Pure Quality?
27. What is Orotund Quality?

LESSON VII

28. **Aspirate Quality is that in which the tone is not vocalized.**

It is suited to expressions of fear, caution, secresy, and some forms of anger and tender emotions. The whisper is the perfection of the Aspirate Quality.

29. **Pectoral Quality is that in which the tone is produced below the natural compass of the voice, and seems to issue from the chest.**

It is suited to expressions of profound awe, despair, malevolence and impersonations of the supernatural and ghostly.

1. Commit the definition of Aspirate Quality.
2. Commit the definition of Pectoral Quality.
3 Learn to what expressions each is adapted.
4 Review the drill on Pure and Orotund Quality.
5. Drill on Aspirate and Pectoral Quality with the following examples.

Effusive.., { Aspirate "Tread softly: bow thy head—in reverent silence bow."
Pectoral—"I am the Grave."

Expulsive { Aspirate—"Boys. be still There's some bad news from Granger's folks."
Pectoral—"List! list! oh list! if ever thou did'st thy dear fatherlove."

Explosive { Aspirate—"But hush! hark! a deep sound strikes like a rising knell!"
Pectoral—"Hell hath no greater torments for the accursed."

QUESTIONS.
28. What is Aspirate Quality?
29. What is Pectoral Quality?

LESSON VIII.

30. The Guttural Quality is that in which the tone is produced in the throat.

It is suited to expressions of dislike, ill-humor, hatred and contempt.

31. Nasal Quality is that in which the tone is forced through the nasal passages.

It is suited to expressions of mimicry and burlesque.

32. Falsetto Quality is that in which the tone is produced above the natural compass of the voice.

It is also suited to expressions of mimicry and burlesque, when the speaker impersonates children and high female voices.

   1. Commit the definition of Guttural Quality.
   2. Commit the definition of Nasal Quality.
   3. Commit the definition of Falsetto Quality.
   4. Learn to what expressions each is adapted.
   5. Review the drills of Pure, Orotund, Aspirate, and Pectoral Qualities.
   6. Drill on Guttural, Nasal and Falsetto Qualities with the following examples:

Effusive...
  Guttural—"Oh! I could curse him too!"
  Nasal —"The birds can fly and why can't I?"
  Falsetto — Now, Caudle, dear! What a man you are!

Expulsive
  Guttural—"Tell me I hate the bowl? Hate is a feeble word."
  Nasal — { They might 'a' knowed wings made o' wax / Would n't stand sun-heat an' hard whacks.
  Falsetto —"I hate to hear everything vulgurly my'd."

Explosive
  Guttural—"Thou slave! thou wretch! thou coward! thou little valiant great in villainy!"
  Nasal —
  Falsetto—"What did you say? Twenty fiddlesticks?"

QUESTIONS.

30. What is Guttural Quality?
31. What is Nasal Quality?
32. What is Falsetto Quality?

LESSON IX.

33. Modulation.
{ Pitch.
| Force.
| Stress.
| Rate.
| Slide.

34. Modulation is the proper variation of the voice.

35. The divisions of Modulation are Pitch, Force, Stress, Rate and Slide.

> " 'Tis not enough the voice be sound and clear,
> 'Tis *modulation* that must charm the ear."

It is Modulation that destroys monotony and renders reading and speaking natural and musical. Without it they become lifeless drawlings. The mind must be filled with all the emotions conveyed by a thorough knowledge of a selection, then only can the voice respond with all its power and beauty, by natural and proper modulation in portraying the feeling of the soul.

36. Pitch. { High. Middle. Low.

37. Pitch is the degree of highness or lowness of ths voice.

38. The divisions of Pitch are High, Middle and Low.

The different degrees of Pitch are produced by the different degrees of tension of the vocal cords. There are three positive degrees of Pitch, and an indefinite number of relative pitches — as many as the compass of the voice will admit. While some have classed Pitch as very high, it is still as undefinite as high; for the pitch might still be higher than very high, until it reaches the very highest of which the voice is capable; so with the classification very low, it may still be lower until it reaches the very lowest of which the voice is still capable.

39. High Pitch is that which is higher than the ordinary key tone of the voice.

High Pitch is adapted to expressions of command, calling, alarm, terror, gayety, ecstatic joy, victory, extreme grief, laughter and courage.

40. Middle Pitch is that which is on the ordinary key tone of the voice.

It is adapted to expressions of ordinary conversation, plain description and simple narrative.

41. Low Pitch is that which is lower than the ordinary key tone of the voice.

It is adapted to expressions of melancholy, soliloquy, devotion, awe and despair.

The judgment and taste must be exercised in applying the various shades of Pitch. The intensity of feeling must be determined before the proper expressions can be given.

   1. Learn the outline of Modulation.
   2. Commit the definition of Modulation.
   3. Learn the divisions of Modulation.

4. Read carefully the explanation of Modulation.
5. Learn the outline of Pitch.
6. Commit the definition of Pitch.
7. Learn the divisions of Pitch.
8. Commit the definitions of High, Middle and Low Pitch.
9. Learn to what expressions each kind of Pitch is adapted.
10. Read carefully what is said in explanation of the degrees of Pitch.
11. Drill on Pitch with the following examples:

High...... { Expulsive—Orotund—"Ah, gentlemen, that was a dreadful mistake."
{ Explosive—Pure—"I come, I come! Ye have called me long."

Middle.. { Effusive...—Pure—The Lord is my shepherd, I shall not want.
{ Expulsive—Guttural—"I loathe, abhor, my very soul with strong disgust is stirred."

Low...... { Effusive...—Orotund—"Roll on! thou ever dark and deep blue ocean, roll."
{ Explosive—Aspirate—"The Greek! the Greek! they come, they come."

QUESTIONS.

33. Place the outline of Modulation on the blackboard.
34. What is Modulation? 35. What are the divisions of Modulation?
36. Place the outline of Pitch on the blackboard.
37. What is Pitch? 38. What are the divisions of Pitch?
39. What is High Pitch? 40. What is Middle Pitch? 41. What is Low Pitch?

LESSON X.

42. Force... { Strong.
{ Moderate.
{ Subdued

43. Force is the degree of energy used in producing tone.

44. There are three degrees of Force: Strong, Moderate and Subdued.

Care should be taken not to confound Pitch with Force. The tension of the vocal cords produce the different degrees of Pitch, while the energy with which the breath is forced through the vocal cords produces the different degrees of Force.

The suggestions concerning the additional classes of Pitch given by some authors will apply also to the additional classes of Force given by them.

45. Strong Force is that which is greater than the ordinary energy of the voice.

It is suited to expressions of defiance, anger, contempt, intense hatred, alarm, terror, shouting, calling, rejoicing, laughter, oratory and courage.

46. Moderate Force is the ordinary energy of the voice.

It is suited to the expressions of reverence, sublimity, devotion, narrative, descriptive and didactic.

47. Subdued Force is that which is less than the ordinary energy of the voice.

It is suited to expressions of tenderness, languor, pathos, melancholy and feebleness.

1. Learn the outline of Force.
2. Commit the definition of Force.
3. Learn the divisions of Force,
4. Read carefully what is said in explanation of Force.
5. Commit the definitions of Strong Force, Moderate Force and Subdued Force.
6. Learn to what expressions each kind of Force is adapted.
7. Drill on Force with the following examples :

Strong .....
: Expulsive—Orotund—High—"Three millions of people armed in the holy cause of liberty."
: Explosive—Guttural—Middle—"Here I fling hatred and full defiance in your face."

Moderate.
: Effusive—Orotund—Low—Bless the Lord, O my soul!
: Expulsive—Pure—Middle—"A few drops of water more or less prostrated Napoleon."

Subdued..
: Effusive—Pure—Middle—"The curfew tolls the knell of parting day."
: Expulsive—Aspirate—Low—"'Twere better by far to have married our fair cousin with young Lochinvar."

QUESTIONS.

42. Place the outline of Force on the blackboard.
43. What is Force?   44. What are the divisions of Force?
45. What is Strong Force?
46. What is Moderate Force?
47. What is Subdued Force?

LESSON XI.

48. Stress...
1. Sustained.
2. Initial.
3. Final.
4. Compound.
5. Swell.
6. Tremulous.

49. Stress is that emphasis of the voice by which one or more words of a sentence are distinguished from the rest.

50. There are six kinds of Stress—Sustained, Initial, Final, Compound, Swell and Tremulous.

Stress may be either absolute or relative; that is, it may be applied independently of any comparison or contrast with other words, or it may depend upon comparison or contrast of different parts of a sentence.

51. Sustained Stress is that in which the emphasis continues throughout the entire word.

It is adapted to expressions of courage, defiance, alarm, terror and command.

52. Initial Stress is that in which the emphasis is placed at the beginning of a word and gradually diminishes.

It is adapted to expressions of oratory, sublimity, description, narration, joy and laughter.

53. Final Stress is that in which the emphasis is gradually augmented from the beginning of a word.

It is adapted to expressions of deep earnestness, horror, intense fear and rage.

54. Compound Stress is a union of Initial and Final.

It is suited to expressions of scorn, contempt, sarcasm and hate.

55. Swell Stress is a union of Final and Initial.

It is adapted to expressions of secret and solemn thought, repose, wailing and longing.

56. Tremulous Stress is that in which the voice is regularly and rapidly intermitted.

It is adapted to expressions of feebleness, deep and suppressed grief, languor and remorse.

1   Learn the outline of Stress.
2. Commit the definition of Stress.
3. Learn the kinds of Stress.
4. Commit the definition of Sustained Stress.
5. Commit the definition of Initial Stress.
6. Commit the definition of Final Stress.
7. Commit the definitions of Compound, Swell and Tremulous Stress.
8. Drill on Stress with the following examples:

Stress.	Form.	Quality.	Pitch.	Force.	EXAMPLES.
Sustained..	Effusive...	Pure ..	High ..	Strong....	Co'boss! eo'boss! eo'! eo'! eo'!
Initial. ...	Expulsive.	Orotund.	High ...	Moderate..	"I know of no way of judging the future but by the past."
Final..	Expulsive.	Orotund.	Middle.	Moderate.	"We may now pause before that splendid prodigy, which towered above us like some ancient ruin."
Compound.	Explosive.	Guttural.	Middle..	Strong.	"Banished from Rome! What's banished but set free?"
Swell......	Effusive...	Pure....	Low. ...	Moderate..	"O, that I had the wings of a dove, that I might fly away and be at rest!"
Tremulous.	Effusive...	Pure ..	Low....	Subdued..	"Pity the sorrows of a poor old man, whose trembling footsteps have borne him to your door "

QUESTIONS.

48. Place the outline of Stress on the blackboard.
49. What is Stress? 50. What are the divisions of Stress?
51. What is Sustained Stress? 52. What is Initial Stress?
53. What is Final Stress? 54. What is Compound Stress?
55. What is Swell Stress? 56. What is Tremulous Stress?

LESSON XII.

57. Rate. $\begin{cases} 1. & \text{Rapid.} \\ 2. & \text{Medium.} \\ 3. & \text{Slow.} \end{cases}$

58. Rate is the degree of fastness or slowness of the voice

59. There are three positive degrees of Rate--Rapid, Medium and Slow.

As with Pitch and Force, there may be an indefinite number of Rates.

60. Rapid Rate is that in which the utterance is faster than in ordinary conversation.

It is suited to expressions of joy, mirth and excitement, quick changes of scene and action, and other expressions of haste.

61. Medium Rate is that which is used in ordinary conversation.

It is suited to expressions of narrative, descriptive and didactic thought.

3

62. Slow Rate is that which is slower than ordinary conversation.

It is suited to expressions of devotion, reverence, solemnity, slow movements and unanimated thought.

1. Learn the outline of Rate.
2. Commit the definition of Rate.
3. Learn the divisions of Rate.
4. Commit the definitions of Rapid, Medium and Slow Rate.
5. Learn to what expressions each class of Rate is adapted.
6. Drill on Rate with the following examples:

Rate.	Form.	Quality.	Pitch.	Force.	Stress.	EXAMPLES.
Rapid....	Expulsive.	Pure..	Middle	Strong...	Initial.	Then there was mounting in hot haste; the steed, The mustering squadron, and the clattering car Went pouring forward with impetuous speed, And swiftly forming in the ranks of war.
Medium .	Effusive...	Pure..	Middle	Moderate	Final .	"Full many a gem of purest ray serene, The dark, unfathomed caves of ocean bear; Full many a flower is born to blush unseen And waste its sweetness on the desert air."
Slow.	Effusive...	Pure..	Low...	Subdued	Swell..	"By Nebo's lonely mountain, On this side of Jordan's wave, In a vale in the land of Moab, There lies a lonely grave."

QUESTIONS.

57. Place the outline of Rate on the blackboard.
58. What is Rate?
59. What are the divisions of Rate?
60. What is Rapid Rate?
61. What is Medium Rate?
62. What is Slow Rate?

LESSON XIII.

63. Slide. $\begin{cases} \text{Upward.} \\ \text{Downward.} \\ \text{Circumflex.} \end{cases}$

64. Slide is a gradual change of Pitch.

65. There are in fact but two Slides of the voice   rising and falling; all others are but modifications of the two.

66. Upward Slide is that in which the voice glides from a lower to a higher key.

67. Downward Slide is that in which the voice glides from a higher to a lower key.

68. Circumflex Slide is a combination of Upward and Downward.

It is adapted to expressions of irony, scorn, doubt and hypothesis.

69. The Monotone is an absence of Slide.

It is adapted to language expressing solemnity and sublimity.

1. Learn the outline of Slide.
2. Commit the definition of Slide.
3. Learn the kinds of Slide.
4. Commit the definitions of Upward, Downward and Circumflex Slide
5. Learn to what expressions Circumflex Slide is adapted.
6. Read carefully what is said in explanation of Monotone.
7. Drill on Slide with the following examples:

Slide.	Form.	Quality.	Pitch.	Force.	Stress.	Rate.	EXAMPLES.
Upward...	Expulsive.	Guttural	Middle .	Strong .	Final....	Medium.	"Has Cassius lived to be but mirth and laughter to his Brutus?"
Downward.	Expulsive.	Orotund.	Middle .	Moderate	Initial ..	Medium.	"It is natural for man to indulge in the illusions of hope."
Circumflex.	Expulsive.	Falsetto.	High ...	Strong ..	Compound.	Rapid...	"Besides, he'd have better taken cold than take our only umbrella."

QUESTIONS.

63. Place the outline of Slide on the blackboard.
64. What is Slide?   65. What are the divisions of Slide?
66. What is Upward Slide?
67. What is Downward Slide?.
68. What is Circumflex?   69. What is Monotone?

LESSON XIV.

70. Gesture. $\begin{cases} \text{1. Attitude.} \\ \text{2. Movements.} \\ \text{3. Facial Expression.} \end{cases}$

71. Gesture is any harmonious action expressive of sentiment and emotion.

72. The divisions of Gesture are Attitude, Movement and Facial Expression.

Speech appeals to the ear, but Gesture appeals to. the eye. Without Gesture man is only a speaking machine. The correct utterance, distinct articulation, perfect modulation, proper emphasis and musical cadence lose much of their beauty and force, if not accompanied by an easy attitude, graceful movements, and suitable expressions of countenance. "Suit the action to the word" is but to "hold the mirror up to nature." The perfect elocutionist must combine harmonious sound with graceful action.

73. Attitude .
$$\begin{cases} \text{1. Firm.} \\ \text{2. Relaxed.} \\ \text{3. Advanced.} \\ \text{4. Retired.} \end{cases}$$

74. Attitude is the posture or position of the body in representing emotion.

75. There are four kinds of Attitude — Firm, Relaxed, Advanced and Retired.

76. Firm Attitude is that in which the body is erect and the muscles are fixed and rigid.

It is adapted to language denoting courage, defiance, boldness, sublimity, commanding, independence and pride.

77. Relaxed Attitude is that in which the muscles are in a loose or slackened condition.

It is suited to language expressing languor, fatigue, horror, intense fear, amazement, disinterestedness, and unemotional language generally.

78. Advanced Attitude is that in which the body is inclined forward.

It is adapted to listening, peering into, hailing, welcome, intense interest, devotion, presentation, caution and humility.

79. Retired Attitude is that in which the body assumes a receding posture.

It is adapted to language denoting disdain, defiance, aversion and abhorrent repulsion.

   1. Learn the outline of Gesture.
   2. Commit the definition of Gesture.
   3. What are the divisions of Gesture.
   4. Read carefully what is said in explanation of Gesture.
   5. Learn the outline of Attitude.
   6. Commit the definition of Attitude.
   7. Learn the kinds of Attitude.

8. Commit the definitions of Firm, Relaxed, Advanced and Retired Attitude.

9. Learn to what expressions each kind is adapted.

10. Drill on Attitude with the following examples:

Firm —"Glory, honor and power be unto him that sitteth on the throne."

Relaxed —"Their spirits were depressed with the weight of adversity."

Advanced — { " Deep into the darkness peering, long I stood there — wondering fearing."

Retired —"Hence! horrible shadow—unreal mockery, hence!"

QUESTIONS.

70. Place the outline of Gesture on the blackboard.
71. What is Gesture?   72. What are the divisions of Gesture?
73. Place the outline of Attitude on the blackboard.
74. What is Attitude?   75. What are the kinds of Attitude?
76. What is Firm Attitude?   77. What is Relaxed Attitude?
78. What is Advanced Attitude!   79. What is Retired Attitude?

LESSON XV.

80. Movement... { Head. Upper Limbs. Lower Limbs.

81. Movement is a change of position, expressive of sentiment or emotion.

82. There are three classes of Movements — of the Head, Upper Limbs and Lower Limbs.

83. Head.... { Erect. Inclined Back. Inclined Forward. Inclined to Side. Listening. Obliquely Back.

An Erect position denotes firmness, manliness and courage.

The Head is Inclined Back in sublime flights of eloquence.

The Head is Inclined Forward in deep reflection and recollection, also in humiliation and shame.

The Head is Inclined to Side in pathetic appeal.

The Head assumes a Listening position in efforts to hear.

The Head is thrown Obliquely Back in light calculation, disgust and abhorrence.

Proper Gestures of the Head are made in natural response to the feelings of the breast. It takes no special drill to secure proper movements of the Head. The drill is required to correct the habit some have of continually nodding, as if to signify approval, or give stress to what is read or spoken.

1. Learn the outline of Movement.
2. Commit the definition of Movement.
3. Learn the classes of Movement.
4. Learn the outline of Head Movements.
5. Learn to what expressions each movement of the Head is adapted.
6. Read carefully what is said in explanation of Head Movements.
7. Drill on Head Movements with the following examples:

Erect —"Ye stand here now like giants, as ye are."

Inclined Forward. { "Other friends have flown before. On the morrow he will leave me, as my hopes have flown before."

Inclined Back — Hail holy light, offspring of heaven's first born.

Inclined to Side. { "Now, Caudle dear! What a man you are! I know you will give me the money."

Listening —"Whence comes those shrieks, so wild and shrill?"

QUESTIONS.

80. Place the outline of Movement on the blackboard.
81. What is Movement?
82. What are the classes of Movement?
83. Place the outline of Head Movements on the blackboard

LESSON XVI.

84. Upper Limbs. { Direction.
Position of Hand.
Position of Arm.
Kinds.

85. Movements of the Upper Limbs includes Gesture made by the Hands and Arms.

86. The divisions of Upper Limb Movements are Direction, Position of Hand, Position of Arm and Kind.

87. Direction. { Straight Lines.
Curved Lines.

88. The Movements of the Upper Limbs are in Straight lines and Curves.

Straight line Movements are adapted to forcible, energetic and bold expressions.

Curved line Movements are adapted to subdued, pathetic, beautiful and sublime expressions.

89. Positions of the Hand. $\begin{cases} \text{Ordinary.} \\ \text{Special.} \end{cases}$

90. The Positions of the Hand are Ordinary and Special.

Ordinary Positions of the Hand are those most commonly used in all varieties of discourse.

Special Positions of the Hand are those used in directing special attention to any object or assertion, or in unusually strong feeling.

91. Ordinary Positions... $\begin{cases} \text{Prone.} \\ \text{Supine.} \end{cases}$

92. The Ordinary Positions of the Hand are Prone and Supine.

93. Prone Position is that in which the palm is downward, the fingers slightly curved.

It is used to indicate super-position, or the resting of one object, part or principle upon another, and to show treachery, concealment and moral and physical destruction.

94. Supine Position is that in which the palm is turned upward.

It is to indicate naked truths, bare thought, intellectual ideas, and the holding up for example.

It will be noticed that the Prone indicates covering up, closing over, concealment; and the Supine, revelation, exposition, giving out.

95. Special Positions... $\begin{cases} \text{Vertical.} \\ \text{Indexical.} \\ \text{Clenched.} \\ \text{Clasped.} \end{cases}$

96. Vertical Position is that in which the fingers point upward.

It is used in repulsion, depreciation, horror, surprise, amazement, pity and solemn obligation.

97. Indexical Position is that in which the index finger is extended, the others being closed.

It is used in close and emphatic designation and discrimination, and to point out distinctly.

98. Clenched Position is that in which the hand is tightly closed.

It is used in fierce determination, desperate resolve, vehement declaration and threatening violence.

99. Clasped Position is that in which the hands are locked together.

It is used in supplication and earnest entreaty.

   1. Learn the outline of Upper limb Movement.

   2. Commit the definition of Upper limb Movement.

   3. Learn the divisions of Upper limb Movements.

   4. Learn the outline of Direction.

   5. Commit the classes of Direction of Upper limb Movements.

   6. Learn to what expressions Straight and Curved line Movements are adapted.

   7. Learn the outline of Position of the Hand,

   8. Learn the general classes of Position of the Hand.

   9. Read carefully what is said in explanation of Ordinary and Special Positions of the Hand.

   10. Learn the outline of Ordinary Positions of the Hand.

   11. Learn the classes of Ordinary Positions.

   12. Commit the definition of Prone and Supine Positions.

   13. Learn to what expressions the Prone and Supine Positions are adapted.

   14. Learn the outline of Special Position,

   15. Commit the definitions of Vertical, Indexical, Clenched and Clasped Positions.

   16. Learn to what expressions each Position is adapted.

   17. Drill on Position of the Hand with the following examples:

Ordinary. $\begin{cases}\text{Prone} \text{—" Green be the turf above thee."} \\ \text{Supine} \text{—" Truth, honor and justice were his motives."}\end{cases}$

Special..... $\begin{cases}\text{Vertical—" Sir, before God I believe the hour has come."} \\ \text{Indexical—" In yonder grave a Druid lies."} \\ \text{Clenched—" I will resist unto death."} \\ \text{Clasped—" O, our Father of mercy, forgive."}\end{cases}$

QUESTIONS.

84. Place on the blackboard the outline of Upper limb Movements.

85. What do movements of the upper limbs include?

86. What are the divisions of Upper limb Movements?

87. Place the outline of Direction on the blackboard.

88. What are the directions of the Upper limb Movements?

89. Place the outline of Positions of the Hand on the blackboard.

90. What are the general Positions of the Hand?

91. Place the outline of Ordinary Positions on the blackboard.

92. What are the Ordinary Positions of the Hand?

93. What is Prone Position?   94. What is Supine Position?

95. Place the outline of Special Positions on the blackboard.

96. What is Vertical Position?   97. What is Indexical Position?

98. What is Clenched Position?

99. What is Clasped Position?

LESSON XVII.

100. Positions of Arm. $\begin{cases} \text{Primary.} \\ \text{Secondary.} \end{cases}$

101. The two classes of Positions of the Arm are Primary and Secondary.

By Primary Positions are meant those simple and general positions which form the basis of classification.

102. Primary Positions. $\begin{cases} \text{Horizontal.} \\ \text{Ascending.} \\ \text{Descending.} \end{cases}$

103. The three Primary Positions are Horizontal, Ascending and Descending.

104. Horizontal Position is that in which the arm is horizontal with the shoulder.

It is adapted to general thought, philosophical narrative and description, and appeals to the intellect.

105. Ascending Position is that in which the arm ascends from the shoulder.

It is adapted to sublime thought and eloquent discourse, and appeals to the imagination.

106. Descending Position is that in which the arm descends from the shoulder.

It is adapted to resolute and emphatic assertion, vehement argument and determination of purpose, and appeals to the will.

107. Secondary Positions.. $\begin{cases} \text{Front.} \\ \text{Front Oblique.} \\ \text{Lateral.} \\ \text{Back Oblique.} \end{cases}$

Secondary Positions are those which are dependent on the Primary.

108. The four Secondary Positions are — Front, Front Oblique, Lateral and Back Oblique.

109. The Front Position is that in which the arm is extended directly in front.

Whether *horizontal, ascending* or *descending,* it is adapted to direct appeal, where the range of thought is confined to a narrow scope.

110. The Front Oblique Position is that in which the arm is extended at an angle of forty-five degrees from the front.

Whether horizontal, ascending or descending, it is adapted to language less emphatic and broader in scope than the Front.

4

111. Lateral Position is that in which the arm is extended directly from the side.

Whether horizontal, ascending or descending, it is adapted to language o a general character, and is in harmony with the broadest scope of thought.

112. Back Oblique Position is that in which the arm extends backwards forty-five degrees.

Whether horizontal, ascending or descending, it is adapted to language referring to the past and remoteness of thought

In Gesture with the Upper Extremities, the shoulder should be made the center of motion, and the movements, through great or small space, quick or slow action, should be commensurate with the character of the discourse and realm of thought.

113. Kinds. { Single. Double.

The Gesture of the Upper Extremities are of two kinds—Single and Double.

When one arm is used, the Gesture is called Single, and when both are used it is called Double.

In Single Gesture perference should always be given to the right arm, and only when reference is made to objects or persons on the *left* should that arm be used.

In Double Gesture the same position of the arms should be observed, and they should be brought into action simultaneously. The Double Gesture denotes stronger feeling than the Single.

1. Learn the outline of Positions of the Arm.
2. Learn the general classes of Positions of the Arm.
3. Learn the outline of Primary Positions.
4. Learn the three Primary Positions of the Arm.
5. Commit the definitions for Horizontal, Ascending and Descending Positions.
6. Learn to what characters of thought each Position is adapted
7. Learn the outline of Secondary Positions.
8 Learn the classes of Secondary Positions.
9. Commit the definition of each Position.
10. Learn to what expressions each is adapted.
11. Read carefully what is said of Positions of the Arm.
12 Learn the outline of Kinds of Movements.
13. Read carefully what is said in explanation of the Kinds.
14. Drill on Positions of the Arm with the following examples:

Horizontal .. { Front—"I appeal to you, Mr. President."
Front Oblique—"These seem to be your sentiments, sirs."
Lateral—"All men are created equal."
Back Oblique—Away back in the history of the past I find it written.

Ascending... { Front—"Thou art my Father and my God."
Front Oblique—"Ye crags and peaks, I am with you once again."
Lateral—"And robes the mountain in its azure hue."
Back Oblique—"The sunset of life gives me mystical lore."

Descending. { Front—" The war is inevitable."
Front Oblique—"What is done cannot be undone."
Lateral—" Thou canst not then be false to any man "
Back Oblique—Get thee behind me, Satan.

QUESTIONS.

100. Place the outline of Positions of the Arm on the blackboard
101. What are the general classes of positions of the Arm?
102. Place the outline of Primary Positions on the blackboard.
103. What are the three Primary Positions?
104. What is the Horizontal Position?
105. What is the Ascending Position?
106. What is the Descending Position?
107. Place the outline of Secondary Positions on the blackboard
108. What are the four Secondary Positions?
109. What is Front Position? 110. What is Front Oblique Position?
111. What is Lateral Position? 112. What is Back Oblique Position?
113. Place the Kinds of Position of the Arm on the blackboard

---

LESSON XVIII.

114. Positions of Lower Limbs. { Advanced.
Retired.

115. There are two Positions of the Lower Limbs - Advanced and Retired.

116. The Advanced Position is that in which either foot may be placed forward, the other supporting the body.

117. The Retired Position is that in which either foot may be placed back, the other supporting the body.

By simply changing the support of the body the position of the lower limbs change.

The distance that the feet should be apart varies from four to nine inches, and the angle that should be formed by the position of the feet is ninety degrees in the Advanced and seventy in the Retired. The angle can be determined by drawing a straight line under the sole of each foot, causing them to intersect. It will be observed that advanced position of the lower limbs necessitate a retired attitude of the body, and retired position of the lower limbs an advanced attitude of the body.

118. Facial Expression. {
Smiling.
Frowning.
Rigid.
Sneering.
Placid.
Dejected.
Averted.
Staring.
}

119. Facial Expression has reference to the feeling and emotion conveyed by the expression of the countenance.

120. Some of the Facial Expressions are—Smiling, Frowning, Rigid, Sneering, Placid, Dejected, Averted and Staring.

Not more accurately does the mirror reflect the image of any object presented to it than the countenance reflects what takes place in the mind. It is, indeed, the "mirror of the soul." Every feeling cf pain or pleasure, joy or grief, victory or defeat, finds its way to the surface, and is written in natural and vivid impress upon the face. Every contortion of the features, every contraction of the brow, every compression of the lips, every flash of the eye, expresses some passion or sentiment of the mind. We find the countenance radiant with smiles in courtesy, joy and good humor; we find it clouded in displeasure, suppressed anger, envy, hatred and jealousy; we find it fixed and rigid in determination, courage and resolute despair. It is dejected and softened in sorrow, cast down and averted in shame. The face should be taught to reflect promptly every change of emotion, as the scene changes to suit the action of the stage. The brow, eyes and mouth are the features which must be most prominent in producing proper facial expression, and it is therefore necessary to study the effect produced on the countenance by a change of these features, and what particular passion, feeling or sentiment produces the change.

1 Learn the outline of Positions of Lower Limbs.
2. Learn the Positions of Lower Limbs.
3 Commit the definitions of Advanced and Retired Positions.
4. Read carefully what is said of these Positions.
5. Learn the outline of Facial Expression.
6. Commit the definition of Facial Expression.
7. Learn some of the Facial Expressions.
8 *Study* carefully what is said of various Facial Expressions.
9. Drill on Positions of the Lower Limbs and Facial Expressions with the following examples:

Position of Lower Limbs.. {
| Advanced—"There, there again ! that demon's there,
Crouching to make a fresh attack "
(Change position.)　　Retired —"Deep into the darkness peering, long I
| stood there."

Facial Expression.

Smiling—"I am delighted to see you."

Frowning—"I am amazed that you, my biggest pupil, should be guilty of an act so rude."

Rigid—"Give me the iron, I say, and bind him there."

Sneering—"Has the gentleman done? Has he completely done?"

Placid —"I've wandered to the village, Tom, I've sat beneath the tree."

Dejected—"Alas! my noble boy, that thou shouldst die!"

Averted —"'Twas she herself, sir," sobbed the lad; "I did not mean to be so bad."

Staring —What light through yonder window breaks?"

QUESTIONS.

114. Place the outline for Positions of the Lower Limbs on the blackboard.

115. What are the two Positions of the Lower Limbs?

116. What is the Advanced Position?

117. What is the Retired Position?

118. Place the outline of Facial Expression on the blackboard.

119. What is Facial Expression?

120. What are some of the Facial Expressions?

LESSON XIX.—OUTLINE OF ELOCUTION.

I. Definition.

II. Objects.
- 1. To understand what is read.
- 2. To give proper expression to what is read.
- 3. Mental and physical culture.

III. Principles.

1. Speech.
- 1. Articulation.
  - 1. Vocal Sounds.
  - 2. Breath Sounds.
  - 3. Union Sounds.
- 2. Utterance.
  - 1. Form.
    - 1. Effusive.
    - 2. Expulsive.
    - 3. Explosive.
  - 2. Quality.
    - 1. Pure.
    - 2. Orotund.
    - 3. Aspirate.
    - 4. Nasal.
    - 5. Guttural.
    - 6. Pectoral.
    - 7. Falsetto.
- 3. Modulation.
  - 1. Pitch.
    - 1. High.
    - 2. Middle.
    - 3. Low.
  - 2. Force.
    - 1. Strong.
    - 2. Moderate.
    - 3. Subdued.
  - 3. Stress.
    - 1. Sustained.
    - 2. Initial.
    - 3. Final.
    - 4. Compound.
    - 5. Swell.
    - 6. Tremulous.
  - 4. Rate.
    - 1. Rapid.
    - 2. Medium.
    - 3. Slow.
  - 5. Slide.
    - 1. Upward.
    - 2. Downward.
    - 3. Circumflex.

2. Gesture.
- 1. Attitude.
  - 1. Firm.
  - 2. Relaxed.
  - 3. Advanced.
  - 4. Retired.
  - 1. Head.
    - 1. Erect.
    - 2. Inclined back.
    - 3. Inclined forward.
    - 4. Inclined to side.
    - 5. Listening.
    - 6. Obliquely back.
- 2. Movements.
  - 2. Upper Limbs.
    - 1. Direction.
      - Straight Lines.
      - Curved Lines.
    - 2. Position of hand.
      - Ordinary.
        - Prone.
        - Supine.
        - Vertical.
      - Special.
        - Indexical.
        - Clenched.
        - Clasped.
    - 3. Position of Arm.
      - Primary.
        - Horizontal.
        - Ascending.
        - Descending.
      - Secondary.
        - Front.
        - "Oblique.
        - Lateral.
        - Back.Obl're.
    - 4. Kind.
      - Single.
      - Double.
  - 3. Lower Limbs.
    - Advanced.
    - Retired.
- 3. Facial Expressions.
  - 1. Smiling.
  - 2. Frowning.
  - 3. Rigid.
  - 4. Sneering.
  - 5. Placid.
  - 6. Dejected.
  - 7. Averted.
  - 8. Staring.

Place this outline on the blackboard.
Review the entire subject.

LESSON XX.

DRILL FOR VOCAL CULTURE.

The long sound of the vowels are to be uttered in the manner indicated a number of times each day, until the tone becomes full, smooth and clear, resounding with a ringing sound. Efforts to locate the tone as far down in the chest, without giving it a pectoral quality, should be encouraged, as this will add richness and volume to the voice

a-e-i-o-u,		Effusively.
a-e-i-o-u,	o o o o o •	Expulsively.
a-e-i-o-u,	O O O O O	Explosively.
a-e-i-o-u,		Initial Stress.
a-e-i-o-u,		Final Stress.
a-e-i-o-u,		Sustained Stress.
a-e-i-o-u,		Compound Stress.
a-e-i-o-u,		Swell Stress.
a-e-i-o-u,		Tremulous Stress.

EXAMPLES IN VOCAL EXPRESSION.

[Read each example in all Forms and Qualities.]

1. "Jo. was very glad to see his old friend."
2. "It took Rome three hundred years to die."
3. "The federal Union must be preserved at all hazards."
4. "Ye fat braggart, an' ye call me coward, I'll stab thee!"
5. "Speak the speech, I pray you, as I pronounce it to you, trippingly on the tongue."
6. "Oh! how oft I've walked these hills, and looked up to my God. and blessed him that this land was free!"
7. "I know not what course others may take, but as for me, give me liberty, or give me death!"
8. "Tell me not in mournful numbers,
    Life is but an empty dream."

In the following selections for practice, care has been taken to select such examples as would illustrate one modulation of the voice at a time. Hence it will be found that the modulation indicated at the head of any piece will predominate, though it may not be appropriate throughout. It is therefore recommended that, at first, attention be given only to what is indicated, applying what is learned in previous selection as the student advances. The judgment and taste must guide in applying the principles of elocution.

SELECTIONS FOR PRACTICE.

THE RAINY DAY.

(Effusive Form.)

The day is cold, and dark, and dreary;
It rains, and the wind is never wèary;
The vine still clings to the mouldering wall,
But at every gust the dead leaves fall,
And the day is dark and dreary.

My life is cold, and dark, and dreary;
It rains, and the wind is never wèary;
My thoughts still cling to the mouldering past,
But the hopes of youth fall thick in the blast,
And the days are dark and dreary.

Be still, sad heart! and cease repining;
Behind the clouds is the sun still shining;
Thy fate is the common fate of all,
Into each life some rain must fall,
Some days must be dark and dreary.   *Longfellow.*

THE NATURE OF TRUE ELOQUENCE.

(Expulsive Form.)

True eloquence does not consist in speech.   It can not be brought from far.   Labor and learning may toil for it, but they will toil in vain.   Words and phrases may be marshaled in every way, but they can not compass it.   It must exist in the man, in the subject, and in the occasion.   Affected passion, intense expression, the pomp of declamation, all may aspire after it — they can not reach it.   It comes, if it comes at all, like the out-breaking of a fountain from the earth, or the bursting forth of volcanic fires, with spontaneous, original, native force.   The graces taught in the schools, the costly ornaments and studied contrivances of speech, shock and disgust men, when their own lives, and the fate of their wives, their children, and their country hang on the decision of the hour.   Then words have lost their power, rhetoric is vain, and all elaborate oratory contemptible.   Even genius itself then feels rebuked and subdued, as in the presence of higher qualities.   Then patriotism is eloquent; then self-devotion is eloquent.   The clear conception, outrunning the deductions of logic, the high purpose, the firm resolve, the dauntless spirit, speaking on the tongue, beaming from the eye, informing every feature, and urging the whole man onward, right onward to his object — this, this is eloquence; or, rather, it is something greater and higher than all eloquence: it is action, noble, sublime, God-like action. —*Daniel Webster.*   5

REPLY TO MR. CORRY.
(*Explosive Form*)

The right honorable gentleman has called me "an unimpeached traitor." I ask why not "traitor," unqualified by an epithet? I will tell him : it was because he durst not. It was the act of a coward, who raises his arm to strike, but has not courage to give the blow. I will not call him villain, because it would be unparliamentary, and he is a privy counsellor. I will not call him fool, because he happens to be chancellor of the exchequer. But I say, he is one who has abused the privilege of Parliament and the freedom of debate, by uttering language which, if spoken out of the House, I should answer only with a *blow.* I care not how high his situation, how low his character, how contemptible his speech ; whether a privy counsellor or a parasite, my answer would be a blow.

He has charged me with being connected with the rebels. The charge is utterly, totally and meanly false. Does the honorable gentleman rely on the report of the House of Lords for the foundation of his assertion ? If he does, I can prove to the committee there was a physical impossibility of that report being true. But I scorn to answer any man for my conduct, whether he be a political coxcomb, or whether he brought himself into power by a false glare of courage or not.

I have returned — not as the right honorable member has said, to raise another storm — I have returned to discharge an honorable debt of gratitude to my country, that conferred a great reward for past services, which, I am proud to say, was not greater than my desert. I have returned to protect that Constitution of which I was the parent and founder, from the assassination of such men as the right honorable gentleman and his unworthy associates. They are corrupt, they are seditious, and they, at this very moment, are in a conspiracy against their country. I have returned to refute a libel, as false as it is malicious, given to the public under the appellation of a report of the committee of the Lords. Here I stand, ready for impeachment or trial. I dare accusation. I defy the honorable gentleman ; I defy the government ; I defy their whole phalanx ; let them come forth. I tell the ministers, I will neither give quarter nor take it. I am here to lay the shattered remains of my constitution on the floor of this House, in defense of the liberties of my country.—*H. Grattan.*

A PSALM OF LIFE.
(*Pure Quality.*)

Tell me not in mournful numbers,
    Life is but an empty dream !
For the soul is dead that slumbers,
    And things are not what they seem.

Life is real ! Life is earnest !
    And the grave is not its goal ;
Dust thou art, to dust returnest,
    Was not written of the soul.

Not enjoyment, and not sorrow,
    Is our destin'd end and way,
But to act, that each to-morrow
    Find us farther than to-day.

Art is long, and time is fleeting,
And our hearts, though stout and brave,
Still, like muffled drums, are beating
Funeral marches to the grave.

In the world's broad field of battle,
In the bivouac of life,
Be not like dumb, driven cattle !
Be a hero in the strife !

Trust no future, howe'er pleasant,
Let the dead Past bury its dead !
Act ! — act in the living Present !
Heart within, and God o'er head.

Lives of great men all remind us,
We can make our lives sublime,
And, departing, leave behind us,
Footprints on the sands of time.

Footprints, that perhaps another,
Sailing o'er life's solemn main,
A forlorn and shipwreck'd brother,
Seeing, shall take heart again.

Let us, then, be up and doing,
With a heart for any fate ;
Still achieving, still pursuing,
Learn to labor and to wait.　　　　　*-Longfellow.*

AGAINST WARREN HASTINGS.
(*Orotund Quality.*)

Do we want a tribunal ? My Lords, no example of antiquity, nothing in the modern world, nothing in the range of human imagination, can supply us with a tribunal like this. We commit safely the interests of India and humanity into your hands. Therefore it is with confidence that, ordered by the Commons,

I impeach Warren Hastings, Esquire, of high crimes and misdemeanors.

I impeach him in the name of the Commons of Great Britain in Parliament assembled, whose parliamentary trust he has betrayed.

I impeach him in the name of all the Commons of Great Britain, whose national character he has dishonored.

I impeach him in the name of the people of India, whose laws, rights, and liberties, he has subverted ; whose properties he has destroyed ; whose country he has laid waste and desolate.

I impeach him in the name and by virtue of those eternal laws of justice which he has violated.

I impeach him in the name of human nature itself, which he has cruelly outraged, injured, and oppressed, in both sexes, in every age, rank, situation, and condition of life.—*Burke.*

TELL ON HIS NATIVE HILLS.
(*Orotund Quality.*)

Oh, with what pride I used
To walk these hills, and look up to my God,
And bless him that the land was free ! 'T was free --
From end to end, from cliff to lake, 't was free !
Free as our torrents are that leap our rocks,
And plow our valleys, without asking leave !
Or as our peaks, that wear their caps of snow
In very presence of the regal sun !

How happy was it then ? I loved
Its very storms. Yes, I have sat
In my boat at night, when, midway o'er the lake,
The stars went out, and down the mountain gorge
The wind came roaring. I have sat and eyed
The thunder breaking from his cloud, and smiled
To see him shake his lightnings o'er my head,
And think I had no master save his own !

On yonder jutting cliff, o'ertaken there
By the mountain blast, I 've laid me flat along,
And while gust followed gust more furiously,
As if to sweep me o'er the horrid brink,
And I have thought of other lands, whose storms
Are summer-flaws to those of mine, and just
Have wished me there — the thought that mine was free
Has checked that wish, and I have raised my head,
And cried in thraldom to that furious wind,
Blow on ! – this is the land of liberty !   *Knowles.*

PARRHASIUS AND THE CAPTIVE.
(*Aspirate Quality.*)

Parrhasius stood, gazing forgetfully
Upon his canvas. There Prometheus lay,
Chained to the cold rocks of Mount Caucasus —
The vulture at his vitals, and the links
Of the lame Lemnian festering in his flesh ;
And as the painter's mind felt through the dim,
Rapt mystery, and plucked the shadows forth
With its far-reaching fancy, and with form
And color clad them, his fine, earnest eye
Flash'd with a passionate fire, and the quick curl
Of his thin nostril, and his quivering lip,
Were like the wing'd god's, breathing from his flight.

" Bring me the captive now!
My hand feels skillful, and the shadows lift
From my waked spirit airily and swift,
  And I could paint the bow
Upon the bended heavens around me play
Colors of such divinity to day.

  "Ha! bind him on his back!
Look! — as Prometheus in my picture here!
Quick — or he faints! — stand with the cordial near!
  Now — bend him to the rack!
Press down the poison'd links into his flesh!
And tear agape that healing wound afresh!

  " So — let him writhe! How long
Will he live thus? Quick, my good pencil, now!
What a fine agony works upon his brow!
  Ha! gray-hair'd, and so strong!
How fearfully he stifles that short moan!
Gods! if I could but paint a dying groan!

  " 'Pity' thee! So I do!
I pity the dumb victim at the altar —
But does the robed priest for his *pity* falter?
  I 'd rack thee, though I knew
A thousand lives were perishing in thine —
What were ten thousand to a fame like mine?

  " 'Hereafter!' Ay — *hereafter!*
A whip to keep a coward to his track!
What gave Death ever from his kingdom back
  To check the skeptic's laughter?
Come from the grave to-morrow with that story
And I may take some softer path to glory.

  " No, no, old man! we die
Even as the flowers, and we shall breathe away
Our life upon the chance wind, even as they!
  Strain well thy fainting eye —
For when that bloodshot quivering is o'er,
The light of heaven will never reach thee more.

  " Yet there 's a deathless *name!*
A spirit that the smothering vault should spurn,
And like a steadfast planet mount and burn —
  And though its crown of flame
Consumed my brain to ashes as it shone,
By all the fiery stars! I 'd bind it on!

" Ay — though it bid me rifle
My heart's last fount for its insatiate thirst —
Though every life-strung nerve be madden'd first —
        Though it should bid me stifle
The yearning in my throat for my sweet child,
And taunt its mother till my brain went wild —

        " All — I would do it all —
Sooner than die, like a dull worm, to rot —
Thrust foully into earth to be forgot !
        O heavens ! — but I appall
Your heart, old man ! forgive —— ha ! on your lives
Let him not faint ! — rack him till he revives !

        " Vain — vain — give o'er ! His eye
Glazes apace. He does not feel you now —
Stand back ! I 'll paint the death-dew on his brow !
        Gods ! if he do not die
But for *one* moment — one — till I eclipse
Conception with the scorn of those calm lips !

        " Shivering ! Hark ! he mutters
Brokenly now — that was a difficult breath —
Another ? Wilt thou never come, O Death !
        Look ! how his temple flutters !
Is his heart still ? Aha ! lift up his head !
He shudders — gasps — Jove help him ! -- so -- he's dead.''

    How like a mounting devil in the heart
    Rules the unrein'd *ambition!* Let it once
    But play the monarch, and its haughty brow
    Glows with a beauty that bewilders thought
    And unthrones peace forever. Putting on
    The very pomp of Lucifer, it turns
    The heart to ashes, and with not a spring
    Left in the bosom for the spirit's lip,
    We look upon our splendor and forget
    The thirst of which we perish !   —*N. P. Willis.*

WAX WORK.
(*Nasal Quality.*)

Once on a time, some years ago,
    Two Yankees, from Connecticut,
Were traveling - on foot, of course,
    A style now out of date ;
And, being far away down South,
    It was n't strange or funny,
That they, like other folks, sometimes
    Should be out of money.

So, coming to a thriving place,
  They hired a lofty hall,
And on the corners of the streets
  Put handbills, great and small,
Telling the people, far and near,
  In printed black and white,
They 'd give a show of *wax work*
  In the great town-hall that night.

Of course the people thought to see
  A mighty show of figures,
Of Napoleon, Byron, George the Third,
  And lots of foreign gentlemen ;
Of Mary, Queen of Scots, you know,
  And monks in black and white,
Heroes, peasants, potentates,
  In wax work brought to light.

One of the Yankees had, they say,
  A monstrous mouth,
And nasal twang, with which
  He thought to gull the South ;
Be that as it may — you see
  A fearful noise he made,
Although he talked obscurely,
  And made on all a useless raid.

The other was a handsome man,
  Quite pleasant, and quite fine ;
He had a form of finest mould,
  And straight as any pine.
Indeed, he was a handsome man
  As you will often see,
Much more so than you — or you — or you,
  Like President Grant — *or me.*

This handsome man stood at the door
  To let the people in,
And the way he took the quarters
  And the shillings was a sin ;
And when the time of show had come,
  He a curtain pulled aside.
And our friend, with a monstrous mouth,
  Stood in all his pomp and pride.

And in his brawny hand he held
  A pound or two, or more,
Of *shoemaker's wax*, which he
  Had some time made before.

He began to work it,
    And his audience thus addressed,
And the people looked and listened ;
    Let their great surprise be guessed.

Said he, "My friends, how some folks cheat
    I never could conceive ;
But this is the real wax work,
    For I stoop not to deceive ;
This is your real wax work,
    For your quarters and your twelves.
Ladies and gentlemen, just walk up
    And examine for yourselves."

But when the people saw the joke,
    With anger they turned pale,
Hammer and tongs they came at him,
    To ride him on a rail;
But he had an open window,
    And a ladder to the ground,
And just as he went out of sight,
    He turned himself around.

And, holding up the wax to view,
    Said, with a saucy grin,
"My friends, here 's no deception,
    For I scorn to take you in ;
This is real *wax work*,
    For your quarters and your twelves.
Ladies and gentlemen, please walk up
    And examine for yourselves."

SCENE BETWEEN BRUTUS AND CASSIUS.
(*Guttural Quality.*)

Cas. Must I endure all this?

Bru. All this? ay, more: Fret till your proud heart break :
Go show your slaves how choleric you are,
And make your bondmen tremble. Must I budge?
Must I observe you? must I stand and crouch
Under your testy humor? By the gods,
You shall digest the venom of your spleen,
Though it do split you; for, from this day forth,
I 'll use you for my mirth, yea, for my laughter,
When you are waspish.

Cas. Is it come to this?

Bru. You say you are a better soldier :
Let it appear so; make your vaunting true,
And it shall please me well : For mine own part,

I shall be glad to learn of noble men.

Cas. You wrong me every way : you wrong me. Brutus :
I said an elder soldier, not a better :
Did I say better ?

Bru. If you did, I care not.

Cas. When Cæsar lived, he durst not thus have moved me

Bru. Peace, peace ; you durst not so have tempted him

Cas. I durst not ?

Bru. No.

Cas. What ! durst not tempt him ?

Bru. For your life you durst not.

Cas. Do not presume too much upon my love ;
I may do that I shall be sorry for.

Bru. You have done that you should be sorry for
There is no terror, Cassius, in your threats ;
For I am arm'd so strong in honesty,
That they pass me as the idle wind,
Which I respect not.   I did send to you
For certain sums of gold, which you denied me
For I can raise no money by vile means ;
— I had rather coin my heart,
And drop my blood for drachms, than to wring
From the hard hands of peasants their vile trash
By any indirection.   I did send
To you for gold to pay my legions,
Which you denied me :   Was that done like Cassius ?
Should I have answered Caius Cassius so ?
When Marcus Brutus grows so covetous,
To lock such rascal counters from his friends,
Be ready, gods, with all your thunderbolts,
Dash him to pieces !   · *Shakspear*

THE HAUNTED HOUSE.

(Aspirate and Pectoral Quality.)

Some dreams we have are nothing else but dreams,
    Unnatural, and full of contradictions ;
Yet others of our most romantic schemes
    Are something more than fiction.

It might be only on enchanted ground,
    It might be merely by a thought's expansion,
But in the spirit or the flesh, I found   '
    An old deserted mansion.

A residence for woman, child, and man,
    A dwelling-place and yet no habitation,
A house — but under some prodigious ban
    Of excommunication.

6

No dog was at the theshold, great or small,
    No pigeon on the roof, no household creature —
No cat demurely dozing on the wall —
    Not one domestic feature.

No human figure stirred to go or come ;
    No face looked forth from shut or open casement :
No chimney smoked — there was no sign of home
    From parapet to basement.

O'er all there hung a shadow and a fear ;
    A sense of mystery the spirit daunted,
And said as plain as whisper in the ear—
    The place is haunted.

No sound was heard except from far away
    The ringing of the whitewall's shrilly laughter,
Or now and then the chatter of the jay,
    That Echo murmured after.

The beds were all untouched by hand or tool ;
    No footsteps marked the green and mossy gravel.
Each walk as green as is the mantled pool
    For want of human travel.

Over all there hung a shadow and a fear ;
    A sense of mystery the spirit daunted,
And said as plain as whisper in the ear --
    The place is haunted.

The fountain was a-dry ; neglect and time
    Had marred the work of artisan and mason,
And efts and croaking frogs begot of slime
    Sprawled in the ruined basin.

On every side the aspect was the same,
    All ruined, desolate, forlorn and savage ;
No hand or foot within the precinct came
    To rectify the ravage.

For over all there hung a shadow and a fear ;
    A sense of mystery the spirit daunted,
And said as plain as whisper in the ear -
    The place is haunted.

Howbeit, the door I pushed — or so I dreamed --
    Which slowly, slowly gaped ; the hinges creaking
With such a rusty eloquence, it seemed
    That Time himself was speaking.

The startled bats flew out ; bird after bird ;
    The screech-owl overhead began to flutter,
And seemed to mock the cry that she had heard
    Some dying victim utter !

The very stairs and pictures on the wall,
  Assuming features horrid and terrific,
Hinted some tragedy in that old hall,
  Locked up in hieroglyphic.

For over all there hung a shadow and a fear;
  A sense of mystery the spirit daunted,
And said as plain as whisper in the ear —
  The place is haunted.

Huge drops rolled down the walls as if they wept;
  And where the cricket used to chirp so shrilly
The toad was squatting and the lizard crept
  On that damp hearth so chilly.

There was so foul a rumor in the air,
  The shadow of a presence so atrocious,
No human creature could have feasted there,
  Even the most ferocious.

For over all there hung a shadow and a fear;
  A sense of mystery the spirit daunted,
And said as plain as whisper in the ear —
  The place is haunted.

The death-watch ticked behind the paneled oak.
  Inexplicable tremors shook the arras,
And echoes strange and mystical awoke
  The fancy to embarrass.

Prophetic hints that filled the soul with dread,
  But through one gloomy entrance mostly,
The while some secret inspiration said —
  That chamber is the ghostly!

One lonely ray that glanced upon the bed
  As if with awful aim, direct and certain,
To show the Bloody Hand in burning red,
  Embroidered on the curtain!

What shrieking spirit in that bloody room
  Its mortal frame had violently quitted!
Across the sunbeam with a sudden gloom
  A ghostly shadow flitted.

O'er all there hung a shadow and a fear;
  A sense of mystery the spirit daunted,
And said as plain as whisper in the ear
  The place is haunted!

Hood

MRS. CAUDLE URGING THE NEED OF SPRING CLOTHING.

(*Falsetto Quality.*)

If there 's anything in the world I hate — and you know it — it is asking you for money. I am sure, for myself, I 'd rather go without a thing a thousand times — and I do, the more shame for you to let me!

"What do I want now?" As if you did n't know! I 'm sure, if I 'd any money of my own, I 'd never ask you for a farthing — never! It 's painful to me, gracious knows!

What do you say? "If it 's painful, why so often do it?" I suppose you call that a joke — one of your club-jokes. As I say, I only wish I 'd any money of my own. If there is anything that humbles a poor woman it is coming to a man's pocket for every farthing. It 's dreadful!

Now, Caudle, you hear me, for it is n't often I speak. Pray, do you know what month it is! And did you see how the children looked at church to-day? — like nobody else's children!

"What was the matter with them?" Oh, Caudle! how can you ask? Weren't they all in their thick merinoes and beaver bonnets?

What do you say? "What of it?" What! You'll tell me that you didn't see how the Briggs girls in their new chips turned their noses up at 'em? And you didn't see how the Browns looked at the Smiths, and then at our poor girls, as much as to say, "Poor creatures! what figures for the first of May!"

"You didn't see it"? The more shame for you! I'm sure those Briggs girls — the little minxes! — put me into such a pucker, I could have pulled their ears for 'em over the pew.

What do you say? "I ought to be ashamed to own it"? Now, Caudle, it's no use talking; those children shall not cross over the threshold next Sunday, if they haven't things for the summer. Now mind — they sha'n't; and there's an end of it!

"I'm always wanting money for clothes"? How can you say that? I'm sure there are no children in the world that cost their father so little; but that's it — the less a poor woman does upon, the less she may.

Now, Caudle, dear! What a man you are! I know you will give me the money, because, after all, I think you love your children, and like to see 'em well-dressed. It's only natural that a father should.

"How much money do I want?" Let me see, love. There's Caroline, and Jane, and Susan, and Mary Anne, and —

What do you say? "I needn't count 'em? You know how many there are!" That's just the way you take me up!

Well, how much money will it take? Let me see — I'll tell you in a minute. You always love to see the dear things look like new pins. I know that, Caudle; and though I say it — bless their little hearts! — they do credit to you, Caudle.

"How much?" Now don't be in a hurry! Well, I think, with good pinching — and you know, Caudle, there's never a wife who can pinch closer than I can — I think, with pinching, I can do with twenty pounds.

What did you say? "Twenty fiddle-sticks"?

What! "You won't give half the money!" Very well, Mr. Caudle; I don't care. Let the children go in rags; let them stop from church, and grow up like heathen and cannibals; and then you'll save your money, and, I suppose, be satisfied

What do you say? "Ten pounds enough"? Yes, just like you men; you think things cost nothing for women; but you don't care how much you lay out upon yourselves.

"They only want frocks and bonnets"? How do you know what they want? How should a man know anything at all about it? And you won't give more than ten pounds? Very well. Then you may go shopping with it yourself, and see what *you'll* make of it! I'll have none of your ten pounds, I can tell you no, sir! *D. W. Jerrold.*

THE OLD YEAR AND THE NEW.
(*High Pitch.*)

Ring out, wild bells, to the wild sky,
   The flying cloud, the frosty light,
   The year is dying in the night;
Ring out, wild bells, and let him die.

Ring out the old, ring in the new,
   Ring, happy bells, across the snow :
   The year is going, let him go ;
Ring out the false, ring in the true.

Ring out the grief that saps the mind
   For those that here we see no more ;
   Ring out the feud of rich and poor,
Ring in redress to all mankind.

Ring out a slowly dying cause,
   And ancient forms of party strife ;
   Ring in the nobler modes of life,
And sweeter manners, purer laws.

Ring out false pride in place and blood,
   The civic slander and the spite ;
   Ring in the love of truth and right,
Ring in the common love of good.

Ring in the valiant and the free,
   The larger heart, the kindlier hand ;
   Ring out the darkness of the land ;
Ring in the Christ that is to be.   *Tennyson.*

ON MODULATION.
(*Middle Pitch.*)

'T is not enough the voice be sound and clear,
'T is modulation that must charm the ear.
W... desperate heroes grieve with tedious moan,
And whine their sorrows in a see-saw tone,
The same soft sounds of unimpassion'd woes

Can only make the yawning hearers doze.
The voice all modes of passion can express,
That marks the proper word with proper stress :
But none emphatic can that speaker call
Who lays an equal emphasis on all.

Some o'er the tongue the labor'd measure roll,
Slow and deliberate as the parting toll ;
Point every stop, mark every pause so strong,
Their words like stage processions stalk along.

All affectation but creates disgust ;
And e'en in speaking we may seem too just.
In vain for them the pleasing measure flows,
Whose recitation runs it all to prose ;
Repeating what the poet sets not down,
The verb disjointing from its favorite noun,
While pause, and break, and repetition join
To make a discord in each tuneful line.

Some placid natures fill the allotted scene
With lifeless drawls, insipid and serene ;
While others thunder every couplet o'er,
And almost crack your ears with rant and roar ;
More nature oft, and finer strokes are shown
In the low whisper, than tempestuous tone ;
And Hamlet's hollow voice and fixed amaze,
More powerful terror to the mind conveys
Than he who, swollen with impetuous rage,
Bullies the bulky phantom of the stage.

He who, in earnest, studies o'er his part,
Will find true nature cling about his heart.
The modes of grief are not included all
In the white handkerchief and mournful drawl :
A single look more marks the internal woe,
Than all the windings of the lengthen'd Oh !
Up to the face the quick sensation flies,
And darts its meaning from the speaking eyes :
Love, transport, madness, anger, scorn, despair ;
And all the passions, all the soul is there.   *Lloyd*

WE WATCHED HER BREATHING.
(*Low Pitch.*)

We watched her breathing through the night,
   Her breathing soft and low,
As in her breast the wave of life
   Kept heaving to and fro.

So silently we seemed to speak,
  So slowly moved about,
As we had lent her half our powers
  To eke her living out.

Our very hopes belied our fears,
  Our fears our hopes belied —
We thought her dying when she slept,
  And sleeping when she died.

For when the morn came dim and sad,
  And chill with early showers,
Her quiet eyelids closed — she had
  She had another morn than ours.   *Thomas Hood.*

SPEECH ON THE TRIAL OF A MURDERER.
(*Strong Force.*)

Against the prisoner at the bar, as an individual, I can not have the slightest prejudice. I would not do him the smallest injury or injustice. But I do not affect to be indifferent to the discovery and the punishment of this deep guilt. I cheerfully share in the oprobrium, how much soever it may be, which is cast on those who feel and manifest an anxious concern, that all who had a part in planning, or a hand in executing this deed of midnight assassination, may be brought to answer for their enormous crime at the bar of public justice.

This is a most extraordinary case. In some respects it has hardly a precedent anywhere; certainly none in our New England history. This bloody drama exhibited no suddenly excited, ungovernable rage. The actors in it were not surprised by any lion-like temptation upon their virtue, overcoming it before resistance could begin. Nor did they do the deed to glut savage vengeance, or satiate long-settled and deadly hate. It was a cool, calculating, money-making murder. It was all "hire and salary, and not revenge." It was the weighing of money against life: the counting out of so many pieces of silver against so many ounces of blood.

An aged man, without an enemy in the world, in his own house, and in his own bed, is made the victim of butcherly murder for mere pay. Truly, here is a new lesson for painters and poets. Whoever shall hereafter draw the portrait of murder, if he shall show it as it has been exhibited in an example where such example was least to have been looked for, in the very bosom of our New England society, let him not give it the grim visage of Moloch, the brow knitted by revenge, the face black with settled hate, and the blood-shot eye emitting livid fires of malice; let him draw, rather, a decorous, smooth-faced, bloodless demon; a picture in repose, rather than in action; not so much an example of human nature in its depravity and in its paroxysm of crime, as an infernal nature, a fiend in the ordinary display and development of his character.

The deed was executed with a degree of self-possession and steadiness, equal to the wickedness with which it was planned. The circumstances now clearly in evidence, spread out the whole scene before us. Deep sleep had fallen on the destined victim, and on all beneath his roof. A healthful old man, to whom sleep was sweet; the first sound slumbers of the night held him in their soft but strong embrace. The assassin enters through the window, already prepared, into an unoccupied apartment. With noiseless foot he paces the lonely hall, half lighted by the moon; he winds up the ascent of the stairs, and reaches the door of the chamber. Of this, he moves the lock, by soft and continued pressure, till it turns on its hinges; and he enters, and beholds his victim before him. The room was uncommonly open to the admission of light. The face of the innocent sleeper was turned from the murderer, and the beams of the moon, resting on the gray locks of his aged temple, showed him where to strike. The fatal blow is given! and the victim passes without a struggle or a motion, from the repose of sleep to the repose of death!

It is the assassin's purpose to make sure work; and he yet plies the dagger, though it was obvious that life had been destroyed by the blow of the bludgeon. He even raises the aged arm, that he may not fail in his aim at the heart; and replaces it again over the wound of the poniard! To finish the picture, he explores the wrist for the pulse! He feels it, and ascertains that it beats no longer! It is accomplished. The deed is done. He retreats, retraces his steps to the window, passes out through it as he came in, and escapes. He has done the murder; no eye has seen him, no ear has heard him. The secret is his own, and it is safe!

Ah! gentlemen, that was a dreadful mistake. Such a secret can be safe nowhere. The whole creation of God has neither nook nor corner where the guilty can bestow it and say it is safe. Not to speak of that eye which glances through all disguises, and beholds everything as in the splendor of noon; such secrets of guilt are never safe from detection, even by men. True it is, generally speaking, that "murder will out." True it is, that Providence hath so ordained, and doth so govern things, that those who break the great law of heaven, by shedding men's blood, seldom succeed in avoiding discovery. Especially, in a case exciting so much attention as this, discovery must come, and will come, sooner or later. A thousand eyes turn at once to explore every man, every thing, every circumstance connected with the time and place; a thousand ears catch every whisper; a thousand excited minds intensely dwell on the scene, shedding all their light, and ready to kindle, at the slightest circumstance, into a blaze of discovery.

Meantime, the guilty soul can not keep its own secret. It is false to itself, or rather it feels an irrisistible impulse to be true to itself. It labors under its guilty possession, and knows not what to do with it. The human heart was not made for the residence of such an inhabitant. It finds itself preyed on by a torment, which it does not acknowledge to God nor man. A vulture is devouring it, and it can ask no sympathy nor assistance, either from heaven or earth. The secret which the murderer possesses, soon comes to possess him; and like the evil spirits of which we read, it overcomes him, and leads him whithersoever it will. He feels it beating at his heart, rising to his throat, and demanding disclosure. He thinks the whole world sees it in his face, reads it in his eyes, and almost hears its workings in the very silence of his thoughts. It has become his master. It betrays his discretion, it breaks down his courage, it conquers his prudence. When suspicions from without begin to embarrass him, and the net of circumstances to entangle him, the fatal secret struggles with still greater violence to burst forth. It *must* be confessed, *will* be confessed; there is no refuge from confession but suicide, and suicide is confession.—*Daniel Webster.*

THE CYNIC.

(*Moderate Force.*)

The Cynic is one who never sees a good quality in a man, and never fails to see a bad one. He is the human owl, vigilant in darkness and blind to light, mousing for vermine, and never seeing noble game.

The Cynic puts all human actions into only two classes openly bad and secretly bad. All virtue, and generosity, and disinterestedness, are merely the appearance of good, but selfish at the bottom. He holds that no man does a good thing except for profit. The effect of his conversation upon your feelings is to chill and sear them ; to send you away sour and morose.

His criticisms and inuendoes fall indiscriminately upon every lovely thing, like frost upon the flowers. If Mr. A. is pronounced a religious man, he will reply: yes, on Sundays. Mr. B. has just joined the church : certainly ; the elections are coming on. The minister of the gospel is called an example of diligence : it is his trade. Such a man is generous : of other men's money. This man is obliging : to lull suspicion and cheat you. That man is upright : because he is green.

Thus his eye strains out every good quality, and takes in only the bad. To him religion is hypocrisy, honesty a preparation for fraud, virtue only a want of opportunity, and undeniable purity, asceticism. The livelong day he will cooly sit with sneering lip, transfixing every character that is presented.

It is impossible to indulge in such habitual severity of opinion upon our fellow men without injuring the tenderness and delicacy of our own feelings. A man will be what his most cherished feelings are. If he encourage a noble generosity, every feeling will be enriched by it ; if he nurse bitter and envenomed thoughts, his own spirit will absorb the poison, and he will crawl among men as a burnished adder, whose life is mischief, and whose errand is death.

He who hunts for flowers will find flowers ; and he who loves weeds may find weeds.

Let it be remembered that no man, who is not himself morally diseased, will have a relish for disease in others. Reject then the morbid ambition of the Cynic, or cease to call yourself a man.—*H. W. Beecher.*

THE BRIDGE OF SIGHS.

(*Subdued Force.*)

One more unfortunate,
　Weary of breath,
Rashly importunate,
　Gone to her death !
Take her up tenderly,
　Lift her with care ;
Fashioned so slenderly,
　Young and so fair !

Look at her garments
Clinging like cerements ;
While the wave constantly
　Drips from her clothing ;
Take her up instantly,
　Loving, not loathing.

Touch her not scornfully ;
Think of her mournfully,
　Gently and humanly ;
Not of the stains of her,
All that remains of her
　Now is pure womanly.

Make no deep scrutiny
Into her mutiny
　Rash and undutiful ;
Past all dishonor,
Death has left on her
　Only the beautiful.

Still, for all slips of hers
　One of Eve's family —

Wipe those poor lips of hers
Oozing so clamily.

Loop up her tresses
Escaped from the comb --
Her fair auburn tresses ;
While wonderment guesses
Where was her home ?

Who was her father ?
Who was her mother ?
Had she a sister ?
Had she a brother ?
Or was there a dearer one
Still, and a nearer one
Yet, than all other ?

Alas for the rarity
Of Christian charity
Under the sun !
O, it was pitiful !
Near a whole city full,
Home she had none.

Where the lamps quiver
So far in the river,
With many a light
From window and casement,
From garret to basement,
She stood, with amazement,
Houseless by night.

The bleak wind of March
Made her tremble and shiver ;
But not the dark arch,
Or the black flowing river :
Mad from life's history,
Glad to death's mystery,
Swift to be hurled,
Anywhere, anywhere
Out of the world !

In she plunged boldly —
No matter how coldly
The rough river ran —
Over the brink of it !
Picture it — think of it !
Dissolute man !
Lave in it, drink of it,
Then, if you can !

Take her up tenderly,
Lift her with care ;
Fashioned so slenderly,
Young and so fair !

Ere her limbs, frigidly,
Stiffen too rigidly,
Decently, kindly,
Smooth and compose them ;
And her eyes, close them,
Staring so blindly !
Dreadfully staring
Through muddy impurity,
As if with the daring
Last look of despairing
Fixed on futurity.

Perishing gloomily,
Spurred by contumely,
Cold inhumanity,
Burning insanity,
Into her rest !
Cross her hands humbly,
As if praying, dumbly,
Over her breast !
Owning her weakness,
Her evil behavior,
And leaving, with meekness,
Her sins to her Savior !

— Hood.

SONG OF MOSES.
(*Initial Stress.*)

Then sang Moses and the children of Israel this song unto the Lord, and spake, saying, I will sing unto the Lord, for he hath triumphed gloriously : the horse and his rider he hath thrown into the sea. The Lord is my strength and song, and he is become my salvation : he is my God, and I will prepare him an habitation ; my father's God, and I will exhalt him. The Lord is a man of war : the Lord is his name. Pharaoh's chariots and his host hath he cast into the sea : his chosen captains also are drowned in the Red Sea. The depths have covered them : they sank into the bottom as a stone. Thy right hand, O Lord, is become glorious in power ; thy right hand, O Lord, hath dashed in pieces the enemy, and in the greatness of thine excellency thou hath overthrown them that rose up against thee : thou sentest forth thy wrath, which consumed them as stubble. And with the blast of thy nostrils the waters were gathered together: the floods stood upright as an heap, and the depths were congealed in the heart of the sea. The enemy said, I will pursue, I will over-take, I will divide the spoil ; my lust shall be satisfied upon them ; I will draw my sword, my hand shall destroy them. Thou didst blow with thy wind, the sea covered them : they sank as lead in the mighty waters. Who is like unto thee, O Lord, among the gods ? who is like thee, glorious in holiness, fearful in praises, doing wonders ? Thou stretchedst out thy right hand, the earth swallowed them. Thou in thy mercy hast led forth the people which thou hast redeemed : thou hast guided them in thy strength unto thy holy habitation. The people shall hear, and be afraid : sorrow shall take hold on the inhabitants of Palestina. Then the dukes of Edom shall be amazed ; the mighty men of Moab, trembling shall take hold upon them : all the inhabitants of Canaan shall melt away. Fear and dread shall fall upon them : by the greatness of thine arm they shall be as still as a stone ; till thy people pass over, O Lord, till the people pass over, which thou hast purchased. Thou shalt bring them in, and plant them in the mountain of thine inheritance, in the place, O Lord, which thou hast made for thee to dwell in ; in the sanctuary, O Lord, which thy hands have established. The Lord shall reign for ever and ever. For the horse of Pharaoh went in with his chariots and his horsemen into the sea, and the Lord brought again the waters of the sea upon them : but the children of Israel went on dry land in the midst of the sea.—*Bible*.

MOUNTAINS.
(*Final Stress.*)

Mountains ! who was your Builder ? Who laid your awful foundations in the central fires, and piled your rocks and snow-capped summits among the clouds ? Who placed you in the gardens of the world, like noble altars, on which to offer the sacrificial gifts of many nations ? Who reared your rocky walls in the barren desert, like towering pyramids, like monumental mounds, like giants' graves, like dismantled piles of royal ruins, telling a mournful tale of glory, once bright, but now fled for-ever, as flee the dreams of a midsummer's night ? Who gave you a home in the islands of the sea — those emeralds that gleam among the waves — those stars of ocean that mock the beauty of the stars of night ?

Mountains ! I know who built you. It was God ! His name is written on your foreheads. He laid your corner-stones on that glorious morning when the orchestra of Heaven sounded the anthem of creation. He clothed your high, imperial forms in royal robes. He gave you a snowy garment, and wove for you a cloudy veil of crimson and gold. He crowned you with a diadem of icy jewels ; pearls from the arctic seas ; gems from the frosty pole. Mountains ! ye are glorious. Ye stretch your granite arms away toward the vales of the undiscovered : ye have a longing for immortality.

But, Mountains ! ye long in vain. I called you glorious, and truly ye are : but your glory is like that of the starry heavens — it shall pass away at the trumpet-blast of the angel of the Most High. And yet ye are worthy of a high and eloquent eulogium. Ye were the lovers of the daughters of the gods ; ye are the lovers of the daughters of Liberty and Religion now ; and in your old and feeble age the children of the skies shall honor your bald heads. The clouds of heaven — those shadows of Olympian power, those spectral phantoms of dead Titans — kiss your summits, as guardian angels kiss the brow of infant nobleness. On your sacred rocks I see the footprints of the Creator ; I see the blazing fires of Sinai, and hear its awful voice. I see the tears of Calvary, and listen to its mighty groans.

Mountains ! ye are proud and haughty things. Ye hurl defiance at the storm, the lightning, and the wind ; ye look down with deep disdain upon the thunder-cloud ; ye scorn the devastating tempest ; ye despise the works of puny man ; ye shake your rock-ribbed sides with giant laughter when the great earthquake passes by. Ye stand as giant sentinels, and seem to say to the boisterous billows, " Thus far shalt thou come, and here shall thy proud waves be stayed ! "

Mountains ! ye are growing old. Your ribs of granite are getting weak and rotten : your muscles are losing their fatness ; your hoarse voices are heard only at distant intervals ; your volcanic heart throbs feebly ; and your lava-blood is thickening, as the winters of many ages gather their chilling snows around your venerable forms. The brazen sunlight laughs in your old and wrinkled faces ; the pitying moonlight nestles in your hoary locks ; and the silvery starlight rests upon you like the halo of inspiration that crowned the heads of dying patriarchs and prophets. Mountains ! ye must die. Old Father Time, that sexton of earth, has dug you a deep, dark tomb ; and in silence ye shall sleep after sea and shore shall have been pressed by the feet of the apocalyptic angel, through the long watches of an eternal night. *E. M. Morse*

THE BELLS OF SHANDON.
(*Sustained Stress.*)

With deep affection,
And recollection,
I often think of
  Those Shandon bells,
Whose sounds so wild would,
In days of childhood,
Fling round my cradle
  Their magic spells.

On this I ponder
Were'er I wander,
And thus grow fonder,
  Sweet Cork, of thee,
With thy bells of Shandon,
That sound so grand on
The pleasant waters
  Of the river Lee.

I 've heard bells chiming
Full many a clime in,
Tolling sublime in
  Cathedral shrine,
While at a glib rate,
Brass tongues would vibrate ;
But all their music
  Spoke not like thine.

For memory, dwelling
On each proud swelling
Of thy belfry, knelling
  Its bold notes free,
Made the bells of Shandon
Sound far more grand on
The pleasant waters
  Of the river Lee.

I 've heard bells tolling
Old Adrian's Mole in,
Their thunder rolling
  From the Vatican,—
And cymballs glorious,
Swinging uproarious,
In the gorgeous turrets
  Of Notre Dame :

But thy sounds were sweeter
Than the dome of Peter
Flings o'er the Tiber,
  So solemnly.
Oh ! the bells of Shandon
Sound far more grand on
The pleasant waters
  Of the river Lee.

There 's a bell in Moscow ;
While on tower and kiosk, oh.
Or in Saint Sophia
  The Turkman gets,
And, loud in air,
Calls men to prayer,
From the tapering summit
Of tall minarets.

Such empty phantom
I freely grant them ;
But there 's an anthem
  More dear to me —
'T is the bells of Shandon,
That sound so grand on
The pleasant waters
  Of the river Lee.   —*Mahony.*

CATILINE'S DEFIANCE.

[*Compound Stress.*]

Banished from Rome! What 's banished, but set free
From daily contact of the things I loathe ?
"Tried and convicted traitor!"—Who says this ?
Who 'll prove it, at his peril, on my head ?
Banished?—I thank you for 't. It breaks my chain !
I held some slack allegiance till this hour ;
But now my sword 's my own.

Smile on, my lords.
I scorn to count what feelings, withered hopes,
Strong provocations, bitter, burning wrongs,
I have within my heart's hot cells shut up,
To leave you in your lazy dignities.
But here I stand and scoff you : — here I fling
Hatred and full defiance in your face.
Your consul 's merciful. For all this thanks.
He dares not touch a hair of Catiline.

"Traitor!" I go — but I return. This . . . . trial!
Here I devote your senate! I 've had wrongs,
To stir a fever in the blood of age,
Or make the infant sinew strong as steel.
This day 's the birth of sorrows! — This hour's work
Will breed proscriptions.

Look to your hearths, my lords ;
For there henceforth shall sit, for household gods,
Shapes hot from Tartarus! — all shames and crimes ;
Wan Treachery, with his thirsty dagger drawn ;
Suspicion, poisoning his brother's cup ;
Naked Rebellion, with the torch and ax,
Making his wild sport of your blazing thrones :
Till Anarchy comes down on you like night,
And Massacre seals Rome's eternal grave.

I go — but not to leap the gulf alone.
I go — but when I come, 't will be the burst
Of ocean in the earthquake,— rolling back
In swift and mountainous ruin. Fare you well !
You build my funeral pile ; but your best blood
Shall quench its flame. Back, slaves !
I will return.
George Croly

THE BURIAL OF MOSES.
(*Swell Stress.*)

By Nebo's lonely mountain,
  On this side Jordan's wave,
In a vale in the land of Moab,
  There lies a lonely grave ;
But no man dug that sepulchre,
  And no man saw it e'er,
For the angels of God upturned the sod,
  And laid the dead man there.

That was the grandest funeral
  That ever passed on earth ;
But no man heard the tramping,
  Or saw the train go forth ;
Noiselessly as the daylight
  Comes when the night is done,
And the crimson streak on ocean's cheek
  Grows into the great sun · ·

Noiselessly as the spring-time
  Her crown of verdure weaves,
And all the trees on all the hills

Open their thousand leaves —
So, without sound of music,
 Or voice of them that wept,
Silently down from the mountain crown
 The great procession swept.

Lo ! when the warrior dieth,
 His comrades in the war,
With arms reversed, and muffled drum,
 Follow the funeral car.
They show the banners taken,
 They tell his battles won,
And after him lead his masterless steed,
 While peals the minute gun.

Amid the noblest of the land
 Men lay the sage to rest,
And give the bard an honored place,
 With costly marble dressed,
In the great minster transept,
 Where lights like glories fall,
And the choir sings, and the organ rings
 Along the emblazoned wall.

This was the bravest warrior
 That ever buckled sword ;
This the most gifted poet
 That ever breathed a word ;
And never earth's philosopher
 Traced, with his golden pen,
On the deathless page, truths half so sage,
 As *he* wrote down for men.

And had he not high honor ?
 The hill-side for his pall ;
To lie in state while angels wait,
 With stars for tapers tall ;
And the dark rock pines, like tossing plumes,
 Over his bier to wave ;
And God's own hand, in that lonely land,
 To lay him in the grave —

In that deep grave, without a name,
 Whence his uncoffined clay
Shall break again — O wondrous thought ! —
 Before the judgment day ;
And stand, with glory wrapped around,
 On hills he never trod,
And speak of the strife that won our life,
 With th' incarnate Son of God.

O lonely tomb in Moab's land !
  O dark Beth-peor's hill !
Speak to these curious hearts of ours,
  And teach them to be still.
God hath his mysteries of grace —
  Ways that we can not tell ;
He hides them deep, like the secret sleep,
  Of him he loved so well.   *—C. F. Alexander.*

BINGEN ON THE RHINE.
(*Tremulous Stress.*)

A soldier of the Legion lay dying in Algiers,
There was lack of woman's nursing, there was dearth of woman's tears :
But a comrade stood beside him, while his life-blood ebbed away,
And bent, with pitying glances, to hear what he might say.
The dying soldier faltered, as he took that comrade's hand,
And he said: " I never more shall see my own, my native land;
Take a message and a token, to some distant friends of mine,
For I was born at Bingen,— at Bingen on the Rhine.   .

"Tell my brothers and companions, when they meet and crowd around,
To hear my mournful story, in the pleasant vineyard ground,
That we fought the battle bravely,— and when the day was done,
Full many a corse lay ghastly pale, beneath the setting sun,
And 'mid the dead and dying, were some grown old in wars,   ·
The death-wound on their gallant breasts, the last of many scars;
But some were young,— and suddenly beheld life's morn decline,—
And one had come from Bingen,— fair Bingen on the Rhine !

" Tell my mother that her other sons shall comfort her old age,
For I was aye a truant bird, that thought his home a cage :
For my father was a soldier, and, even as a child,
My heart leaped forth to hear him tell of struggles fierce and wild ;
And when he died, and left us to divide his scanty horde,
I let them take what'ere they would — but kept my father's sword ;
And with boyish love I hung it where the bright light used to shine,
On the cottage wall at Bingen,— calm Bingen on the Rhine !

" Tell my sister not to weep for me, and sob with drooping head,
When the troops are marching home again with glad and gallant tread :
But to look upon them proudly, with a calm and steadfast eye,
For her brother was a soldier, too, and not afraid to die.
And, if a comrade seek her love, I ask her in my name.
To listen to him kindly, without regret or shame ;
And to hang the old sword in its place, (my father's sword and mine).
For the honor of old Bingen — dear Bingen on the Rhine !

"There's another—not a sister;— in the happy days gone by,
You'd have known her by the merriment that sparkled in her eye;
Too innocent for coquetry — too fond for idle scorning ;—
O friend, I fear the lightest heart makes sometimes heaviest mourning !
Tell her the last night of my life —(for ere this moon be risen
My body will be out of pain — my soul be out of prison),
I dreamed I stood with *her*, and saw the yellow sunlight shine
On the vine-clad hills of Bingen — fair Bingen on the Rhine !

"I saw the blue Rhine sweep along — I heard, or seemed to hear,
The German songs we used to sing, in chorus sweet and clear ;
And down the pleasant river, and up the slanting hill,
That echoing chorus sounded, through the evening calm and still ;
And her glad blue eyes were on me, as we passed with friendly talk,
Down many a path beloved of yore, and well-remembered walk ;
And her little hand lay lightly, confidingly in mine :
But we'll meet no more at Bingen — loved Bingen on the Rhine !"

His voice grew faint and hoarser — his grasp was childish weak —
His eyes put on a dying look — he sighed and ceased to speak :
His comrade bent to lift him, but the spark of life had fled —
The soldier of the Legion, in a foreign land — was dead !
And the soft moon rose up slowly, and calmly she looked down,
On the red sand of the battle-field, with bloody corpses strown ;
Yea, camly on that dreadful scene her pale light seemed to shine,
As it shone on distant Bingen — fair Bingen on the Rhine ! —*Mrs. Norton.*

THE BURNING SHIP.
(*Rapid Rate.*)

The storm o'er the ocean flew furious and fast,
And the waves rose in foam at the voice of the blast,
And heavily labored the gale-beaten ship,
Like a stout-hearted swimmer, the spray at his lip ;
And dark was the sky o'er the mariner's path,
Save when the wild lightning illumined in wrath.
A young mother knelt in the cabin below,
And pressing her babe to her bosom of snow,
She prayed to her God, 'mid the hurricane wild,
"O Father, have mercy, look down on my child !"

It passed — the fierce whirlwind careered on its way,
And the ship like an arrow divided the spray ;
Her sails glimmered white in the beams of the moon,
And the wind up aloft seemed to whistle a tune — to whistle a tune.

There was joy in the ship as she furrowed the foam,
For fond hearts within her were dreaming of home.
The young mother pressed her fond babe to her breast,
And the husband sat cheerily down by her side,

And looked with delight on the face of his bride.
"Oh, happy," said he, "when our roaming is o'er,
We 'll dwell in our cottage that stands by the shore.
Already in fancy its roof I descry,
And the smoke of its hearth curling up to the sky;
Its garden so green, and its vine-covered wall;
The kind friends awaiting to welcome us all,
And the children that sport by the old oaken tree."
Ah, gently the ship glided over the sea!
Hark! what was that? Hark! Hark to the shout!
"Fire!" Then a tramp and a rout, and a tumult of voices uprose on
    the air—
And the mother knelt down, and the half-spoken prayer,
That she offered to God in her agony wild,
Was, "Father, have mercy, look down on my child!"
She flew to her husband, she clung to his side,
Oh there was her refuge what e'er might betide.
"Fire!" "Fire!" It was raging above and below—
And the cheeks of the sailors grew pale at the sight,
And their eyes glistened wild in the glare of the light.
'T was vain o'er the ravage the waters to drip;
The pitiless flame was the lord of the ship,
And the smoke in thick wreaths mounted higher and higher.
"O God, it is fearful to perish by fire."
Alone with destruction, alone on the sea,
"Great Father of mercy, our hope is in thee."
Sad at heart and resigned, yet undaunted and brave,
They lowered the boat, a mere speck on the wave.
First entered the mother, enfolding her child:
It knew she caressed it, looked upward and smiled.
Cold, cold was the night as they drifted away,
And mistily dawned o'er the pathway the day;—
And they prayed for the light, and at noontide about,
The sun o'er the waters shone joyously out.

"Ho! a sail! Ho! a sail!" cried the man at the lea,
"Ho! a sail!" and they turned their glad eyes o'er the sea.
"They see us, they see us, the signal is waved!
They bear down upon us, they bear down upon us:
Huzza! we are saved."

BURIAL OF SIR JOHN MOORE.
(*Slow Rate.*)

Not a drum was heard, not a funeral note,
  As his corse to the rampart we hurried;
Not a soldier discharged his farewell shot
  O'er the grave where our hero was buried.

We buried him darkly, at dead of night,
  The sods with our bayonets turning;
By the struggling moonbeam's misty light,
  And the lanterns dimly burning.

No useless coffin enclosed his breast,
  Not in sheet nor in shroud we wound him;
But he lay like a warrior taking his rest,
  With his martial cloak around him.

Few and short were the prayers we said,
  And we spoke not a word of sorrow;
And steadfastly gazed on the face of the dead,
  And we bitterly thought of the morrow.

We thought, as we hollow'd his narrow bed,
  And smooth'd down his lonely pillow,
That the foe and the stranger would tread o'er his head,
  And we far away on the billow.

Lightly they 'll talk of the spirit that 's gone,
  And o'er his cold ashes upbraid him,
But little he 'll reck, if they let him sleep on
  In the grave where a Briton has laid him.

But half of our heavy task was done,
  When the clock struck the hour for retiring;
And we heard the distant random gun
  Which the foe was sullenly firing.

Slowly and sadly we laid him down,
  From the field of his fame fresh and gory;
We carv'd not a line, we rais'd not a stone,
  But left him alone in his glory.   —*Charles Wolf.*

THE RAVEN.

Once upon a midnight dreary, while I ponder'd, weak and weary,
Over many a quaint and curious volume of forgotten lore,
While I nodded, nearly napping, suddenly there came a tapping,
As of some one gently rapping, rapping at my chamber door.
" 'Tis some visitor," I mutter'd, " tapping at my chamber door;
    Only this and nothing more."

Ah! distinctly I remember, it was in the bleak December,
And each separate dying ember wrought its ghost upon the floor;
Eagerly I wish'd the morrow: vainly I had tried to borrow,
From my books, surcease of sorrow — sorrow for the lost Lenore,
For the rare and radiant maiden whom the angels name Lenore,
    Nameless here for evermore.

And the silken, sad uncertain rustling of each purple curtain
Thrill'd me, fill'd me with fantastic terrors, never felt before ;
So that now, to still the beating of my heart, I stood repeating,
" "Tis some visitor entreating entrance at my chamber door,
Some late visitor entreating entrance at my chamber door ;
   This it is and nothing more."

Presently my soul grew stronger, hesitating then no longer,
"Sir," said I, "or Madam, truly your forgiveness I implore ;
But the fact is, I was napping, and so gently you came rapping,
And so faintly you came tapping, tapping at my chamber door,
That I scarce was sure I heard you." Here I opened wide the door.
   Darkness there, and nothing more.

Deep into that darkness peering, long I stood there, wondering, fearing,
Doubting, dreaming dreams no mortal ever dared to dream before,
But the silence was unbroken, and the darkness gave no token,
And the only word there spoken, was the whispered word, "Lenore!"
   Merely this, and nothing more.

Then into the chamber turning, all my soul within me burning,
Soon I heard again a tapping, somewhat louder than before ;
"Surely," said I, "surely, that is something at my window lattice ;
Let me see then, what thereat is, and this mystery explore,
Let my heart be still a moment, and this mystery explore,
   'Tis the wind, and nothing more !"

Open here I flung the shutter, when, with many a flirt and flutter,
In there stepp'd a stately raven of the saintly days of yore :
Not the least obeisance made he ; not an instant stopp'd or stay'd he ;
But with mien of lord or lady, perch'd above my chamber door,
Perch'd upon a bust of Pallas, just above my chamber door,
   Perch'd, and sat, and nothing more.

Then this ebony bird beguiling my sad fancy into smiling,
By the grave and stern decorum of the countenance it wore ;
"Though thy crest be shorn and shaven, thou," I said, "art sure no craven,
Ghastly, grim, and ancient raven, wandering from the nightly shore,
Tell me what thy lorldy name is on the night's Plutonian shore !"
   Quoth the raven, "Nevermore."

Much I marvel'd this ungainly fowl to hear discourse so plainly,
Though its answer little meaning, little revelency bore ;
For we cannot help agreeing that no living human being
Ever yet was bless'd with seeing bird above his chamber door,
Bird or beast upon the sculptur'd bust above his chamber door,
   With such name as "Nevermore."

But the raven, sitting lonely on the placid bust, spake only
That one word, as if his soul in that one word he did out-pour,
Nothing further then he utter'd, not a feather then he flutter'd,

Till I scarcely more than mutter'd, "other friends have flown before,
On the morrow he will leave me, as my hopes have flown before,"
    Then the bird said, "Nevermore."

Startled at the stillness broken by reply so aptly spoken,
"Doubtless," said I, "what it utters is its only stock and store,
Caught from some unhappy master, whom unmerciful disaster,
Follow'd fast and follow'd faster, till his song one burden bore,
Till the dirges of his hope the melancholy burden bore
    Of 'Nevermore,' of 'Nevermore.'"

But the raven still beguiling all my sad soul into smiling,
Straight I wheel'd a cushion'd seat in front of bird, and bust, and door ;
Then upon the velvet sinking, I betook myself to linking
Fancy unto fancy, thinking what this ominous bird of yore,
What this grim, ungainly, ghastly, gaunt, and ominous bird of yore
    Meant, in croaking "Nevermore."

Thus I sat engaged in guessing, but no syllable expressing
To the fowl whose fiery eyes now burn'd into my bosom's core.
This and more I sat divining, with my head at ease reclining,
On the cushion's velvet lining that the lamplight gloated o'er,
But whose velvet violet lining, with the lamplight gloating o'er,
    She shall press, ah, Nevermore !

Then, methought, the air grew denser, perfumed from an unseen censer,
Swung by angels, whose faint foot-falls tinkled on the tufted floor ;
"Wretch," I cried, "thy God hath lent thee, by these angels he hath sent thee
Respite — respite, and nepenthe from thy memories of Lenore !
Quaff, O, quaff this kind nepenthe, and forget this lost Lenore !"
    Quoth the raven, "Nevermore."

"Prophet," cried I, "thing of evil, prophet still, if bird or devil,
Whether tempter sent, or whether tempest toss'd thee here ashore,
Desolate, yet all undaunted, on this desert land enchanted,
On this home by honor haunted — tell me truly, I implore,
Is there, *is* there balm in Gilead, tell me, tell me, I implore,"
    Quoth the raven, "Nevermore."

"Prophet," said I, "thing of evil, prophet still, if bird or devil,
By that heaven that bends above us, by that God we both adore,
Tell this soul with sorrow laden, if within the distant Aiden,
It shall clasp a sainted maiden, whom the angels name Lenore,
Clasp a rare and radiant maiden, whom the angels name Lenore,"
    Quoth the raven, "Nevermore."

"Be that word our sign of parting, bird or fiend !" I shriek'd upstarting ;
"Get thee back into the tempest, and the night's Plutonian shore ;
Leave no black plume as a token of that lie thy soul hath spoken !
Leave my loneliness unbroken ! quit the bust above my door !
Take thy beak from out my heart, and take thy form from off my door."
    Quoth the raven, "Nevermore."

And the raven, never flitting, still is sitting, still is sitting,
On the pallid bust of Pallas, just above my chamber door ;
And his eyes have all the seeming of a demon that is dreaming,
And the lamp-light, o'er him streaming, throws his shadow on the floor ;
And my soul from out that shadow, that lies floating on the floor,
   Shall be lifted, Nevermore !   *—E. A. Poe.*

THE VAGABONDS.

We are two travelers, Roger and I.
 Roger 's my dog :— come here, you scamp !
Jump for the gentlemen — mind your eye !
 Over the table — look out for the lamp ! —
The rogue is growing a little old ;
 Five years we 've tramped through wind and weather,
And slept out-doors when nights were cold,
 And ate and drank — and starved together.

We 've learned what comfort is, I tell you !
 A bed on the floor, a bit of rosin,
A fire to thaw our thumbs (poor fellow !
 The paw he holds up there 's been frozen),
Plenty of cat-gut for my fiddle
 (This out-door business is bad for strings),
Then a few nice buckwheats hot from the griddle,
 And Roger and I set up for kings !

No, thank ye, sir — I never drink ;
 Roger and I are exceedingly moral —
Are n't we, Roger ? — see him wink !—
 Well, something hot, then — we wont quarrel.
He 's thirsty, too — see him nod his head ?
 What a pity, sir, that dogs can 't talk !
He understands every word that 's said —
 And he knows good milk from water-and-chalk.

The truth is, sir, now I reflect,
 I 've been so sadly given to grog,
I wonder I 've not lost the respect
 (Here 's to you, sir!) even of my dog.
But he sticks by, through thick and thin ;
 And this old coat, with its empty pockets,
And rags that smell of tobacco and gin,
 He 'll follow while he has eyes in his sockets.

There is n't another creature living
 Would do it, and prove, through every disaster,
So fond, so faithful, and so forgiving
 To such a miserable, thankless master !

No, sir! — see him wag his tail and grin!
  By George! it makes my old eyes water!
That is, there 's something in this gin
  That chokes a fellow.   But no matter!

We 'll have some music, if you 're willing,
  And Roger (hem! what a plague a cough is, sir!)
Shall march a little. — Start, you villain!
  Stand straight!   'Bout face!   Salute your officer!
Put up that paw!   Dress!   Take your rifle!
  (Some dogs have arms, you see!)   Now hold your
Cap while the gentlemen give a trifle,
  To aid a poor old patriot soldier!

March!   Halt!   Now show how the rebel shakes
  When he stands up to hear his sentence.
Now tell us how many drams it takes
  To honor a jolly new acquaintance.
Five yelps — that 's five; he 's mighty knowing!
  The night 's before us, fill the glasses! —
Quick, sir!   I 'm ill — my brain is going! —
  Some brandy — thank you — there! — it passes!

Why not reform?   That 's easily said;
  But I 've gone through such wretched treatment,
Sometimes forgetting the taste of bread,
  And scarce remembering what meat meant,
That my poor stomach 's past reform;
  And there are times when, mad with thinking,
I 'd sell out heaven for something warm
  To prop a horrible inward sinking.

Is there a way to forget to think?
  At your age, sir, home, fortune friends,
A dear girl's love — but I took to drink; —
  The same old story; you know how it ends.
If you could have seen these classic features —
  You need n't laugh sir; they were not then
Such a burning libel on God's creatures:
  I was one of your handsome men!

If you had seen her, so fair and young,
  Whose head was happy on this breast!
If you could have heard the songs I sung
  When the wine went round, you would n't have guessed
That ever I, sir, should be straying
  From door to door, with fiddle and dog,
Ragged and penniless, and playing
  To you to-night for a glass of grog!

She 's married since — a parson's wife :
  'T was better for her that we should part —
Better the soberest, prosiest life,
  Than a blasted home and a broken heart.
I have seen her — once : I was weak and spent
  On the dusty road — a carriage stopped :
But little she dreamed, as on she went,
  Who kissed the coin that her fingers dropped !

You 've set me talking, sir ; I 'm sorry ;
  It makes me wild to think of the change !
What do you care for a beggar's story ?
  Is it amusing ? you find it strange ?
I had a mother so proud of me !
  'T was well she died before———. Do you know
If the happy spirits in heaven can see
  The ruin and wretchedness here below ?

Another glass, and strong, to deaden
  This pain ; then Roger and I will start.
I wonder, has he such a lumpish, leaden,
  Aching thing, in place of a heart ?
He is sad sometimes, and would weep, if he could,
  No doubt, remembering things that were —
A virtuous kennel, with plenty of food,
  And himself a sober, respectable cur.

I 'm better now ; that glass was warming. —
  You rascal ! limber your lazy feet !
We must be fiddling and performing
  For supper and bed, or starve in the street. —
Not a very gay life to lead, you think ?
  But soon we shall go where lodgings are free,
And the sleepers need neither victuals nor drink ; —
  The sooner, the better for Roger and me !   *J. T. Trowbridge.*

www.ingramcontent.com/pod-product-compliance
Lightning Source LLC
Chambersburg PA
CBHW021523090426
42739CB00007B/756